EUROPE

Frontispiece: Neuschwanstein in Bavaria. Photograph by Ewing Krainin, courtesy of Pan American World Airways.

Europe

A JOURNEY WITH PICTURES

Anne Fremantle
AND
Bryan Holme

FOREWORD BY LEWIS MUMFORD

THE STUDIO PUBLICATIONS, INC.

IN ASSOCIATION WITH THOMAS Y. CROWELL COMPANY

Foreword

LEWIS MUMFORD

During the last quarter of the nineteenth century, Henry James wrote a series of short stories and novels, dealing with the problem of how an American should behave in Europe. In what manner, he repeatedly asked himself, can an outsider come to terms with this complex culture and resolve the differences, sometimes subtle, sometimes blatant, between the European mind, cushioned on a many-layered past, and a modern mind, formed in a new environment without any comparable possessions, except those brought over in ancestral chests. James is still a valuable mentor in Europe, and the dilemmas presented to his heroes and heroines still often occur to the New World visitor. But one of the ways of seeing these difficulties freshly did not occur to James: to realize that the problem of assimilation and intercourse is, after all, a European problem. Europe itself, once Hellenic civilization disintegrated, was taken over by outlanders and colonized afresh by parvenus: the streets of its great cities were filled with Innocents Abroad long before Mark Twain. In the eleventh century European settlers cleared the forests of the north and built pioneer towns, with the same dogged vigor—and much higher esthetic skill—than their later descendants in the New World. There is nothing in our present that has not come up, in some parallel form, in Europe's past. In fact, no embarrassment a Western traveler suffers today in Europe is greater than must have been felt by an imperial Roman sightseeing in Athens or a provincial Celt visiting Rome. Europe is a mystery and a challenge, a puzzling mixture and a problem, a temptation and a delight, even to the European.

Europe is more than a continent or a group of intensely individualized nations and regions: it is like those exposed rock dwellings in the Dordogne, which reveal, ledge by ledge, different stages in the development of civilization. The richness of Europe, then, lies not merely in its past, venerable though it is, but in its capacity for renewal, indeed, its love for newness. The pointed Gothic buildings that we now admire partly because of the patina of age, were, in their own time, highly experimental structures, architectural heresies never before uttered, comparable as engineering feats to the first steel suspension bridges. Even what the European sometimes irritably refers to as "Americanism" is actually as much a part of the European tradition as the monumental aqueducts and sewers of Rome, or the law and order and military discipline that accompanied them. To think of mechanization and quantification as a characteristically American quality is as absurd as to think of the atomic bomb as a specifically American invention. These traits had their origin in the European mind. Indeed, what is America itself, or the New World, but an idea thrown out by Europe, at a moment when the meanings and forms of medieval society had become empty? The immense attraction of Europe lies in the fact that there, as nowhere else, the immemorial but still-living past mingles in the present with the still-emerging future. So the Eiffel Tower (Paris, 1889) or the Festival Hall (London, 1951) is as historic as the medieval Tour Saint Jacques; and the modern railway station at Rome, for all its outward dash, is continuous with the Roman ruins that abut it. The old French observation, "The more it changes, the more it remains the same," has for European culture a reverse twist: the more stable it seems, the more dynamic its creative possibilities. The very age that produced the "final" synthesis of Thomas Aquinas and Dante saw that finality explode into a dozen fragments that have not yet been put together again.

If Europe were just a museum, one might reserve its exploration for collectors and curiosity seekers. At best, it would have the same attraction as a studied piece of historic reconstruction, like our own Williamsburg, laboriously authentic, but a little dull, served by attendants in costume, whose ancient cut is openly contradicted by a twentieth-century face. This is not to say that there are not, here and there in Europe, some painfully arranged moments, some too carefully staged settings. In Venice the gondoliers now sing at night a pitifully limited number of songs, which sound as if the singers had studied at evening school and had not gotten beyond the first week; the naughty gaiety of Montmartre seems to have been arranged by a Hollywood director, rehearsing a scene once too often; and there are noble shrines, like the Sistine Chapel, whose esthetic value is now stifled by their popularity as museum pieces. But even some of the most artfully historic spectacles, staged in costume like the Sienese horse races or the procession of young men in Florence on Saint John's Day, retain some of their boisterous vitality, just as if for the sober young Italians who take part in these pageants it was their drab workaday clothes that were unreal and fantastic, and their colorful renaissance doublets and hose that were still their "real" clothes. In essence, then, Europe is not a museum; indeed, one might say that the habit of putting so much of its valued possessions into museums had its origin in the need to make room for the new forms and activities of later days. Europe is rather a setting for a life full of varied possibilities, because of the constantly maintained interplay of time and space, of the new and the old, the remembered and the anticipated: possibilities so varied, so abundant, so inexhaustible, that no one country or region can hold them, even for a European.

There are two ways of penetrating this wealth of landscapes and peoples. One way is to move rapidly over the land as a sightseer; the other way is to confine oneself to a relatively small area and remain there long enough to penetrate beneath the surface. The first way is perhaps the most tempting, and it is no wonder that the majority of travelers succumb to it. But as sometimes happens to a child beneath a Christmas tree, in the eagerness to uncover Europe's treasures one may spend so much time opening the packages one doesn't have the time or patience to examine the contents. That happens, all too often, on swift, highly organized trips that aim to touch all the high spots, with measured minutes or hours for this shrine, that museum, or the other monument. Long ago I met a nice American couple who were going to Europe for the first time on such a journey; and by accident, a year later, I ran across the husband on Fifth Avenue and asked him how he and his wife had fared. "We had a wonderful trip," he assured me; "actually we managed to see everything we planned to see. But we hope to go over again soon. This time we're going just for pleasure and we'll take our time." How wise were his second thoughts! The advantage of such a book as the present one is that through its pictures and its perceptive comments it gives the reader many of the advantages of a first exploratory trip with none of its drawbacks: no harried early morning awakenings, no glazed-eye alertness at noonday, no melancholy frustration in the evening. And for those who have already explored Europe, a graphic review like this not only evokes precious memories but quickens anticipations of journeys still to come, for the more one knows of Europe the more there remains to see.

Once this first exciting survey of Europe is accomplished by book or by person, one may undertake the more intensive task of courting intimacy, or the beginnings of intimacy; and here one may let whim or chance opportunity, sentiment or dream, guide one; for there is hardly a spot in Europe where one might not, and without moving more than a few miles in any direction, bring to light the whole pageant of human culture, from the glacial period onward: stones, cairns, skeletons, shards, pots, safety pins, swords; tombs, shrines, camps, forts, temples, monuments, castles, palaces, cathedrals, cities. Some of the underlying pessimism of the European may be due to his consciousness of the fact that other peoples and other cultures, as full of great forms and significant values as his own, have occupied the same region and all but vanished. But some of the tough vitality of the European may be due to the fact that, on this same spot, life has gone on, producing new ideas, religions, patterns of personality, forms of art, methods of government. How many different layers of European experience go into the makeup of a Spaniard, an Italian, a Netherlander, a Pole; even episodes that have fallen out of consciousness remain present in his daily environment, in the form of paintings or buildings or country folkways, ready like a seemingly dead ember to glow again at some passing gust of life. As with those ancient churches, built over pagan altars, one finds deposits from many different eras in the psyche of a European: fragments as it were of a Roman arch, a Norman buttress, a Gothic nave, a Renaissance chapel, a niche emptied by Puritan iconoclasm, a nineteenth century restoration, or a bit of makeshift modern heating, capped by a newly fashioned electrolier. Many of these elements, latent if not visibly present, are at work in the mind of a European—though, as in an old building, they may be temporarily hidden by the coat of plaster applied by his profession or his social class. Such people are too complex in their composition to have simple answers to anything. But, though each nationality, indeed each region and city, has a deep sense of its own identity, Europeans meet below the surface, through the intertwining of their historic root systems: it is by this underlying complexity, by this deviousness, by this historic involvement and commitment that they secretly recognize each other. Is it any wonder that they recoil, with an inward smile, from the naive visitors who fancy that what immediately meets the eye is all that need concern the mind? This complex European attitude is the translation, into the spirit, of that rich compost of landscapes and cultures, of ways of historic life and ideals, of forms and images that make up the reality of Europe through its age-old transformation. Even if the visitor is prepared to read and ponder and converse, that mind does not admit strangers lightly into its intimacies. But fortunately, the cities and fields of Europe are in turn the public expression of the European mind as it has confronted Nature and traversed time: so that he who explores them lovingly may penetrate ever closer to the living spirit of Europe.

Europe's deep historic root system perhaps explains its physical vitality, its capacity for withstanding drought and for recovering from storm and stress. Today that vitality astonishes the visitor, wherever he goes. Despite two world wars, with the widespread bombing of its cities, from London to Warsaw, from Naples to Helsinki, so much has already been rebuilt and restored that except for surviving patches of extreme devastation Europe today looks stronger and healthier than ever it did in the nineteenth century, when the new forces of industrialism actually worked even grimmer devastations so positive in character, so massive in form, that they long stood in the way of renewal. Though no small part of the physical means of this recovery doubtless came from the United States, the constructive zeal and skill were Europe's own. If the spiritual rehabilitation of Europe will take more time, before it lives down the shocks and injuries of the last thirty years, one can hardly doubt that this, too, is under way, though few signs of it may yet be visible. Spiritually Europe today is like a pollarded tree, cut back to a few main stems that are widely split, and clumsily held together by iron bands. From Europe's ancient roots, new shoots will come forth, and in time another stem will grow beside the old trunk. So it has been in the past; so it will be again. For though Europe is sustained by the life of the past, it still reaches toward the future; and renewed youth may once more be the portion of the continent where Western man first made the future, as ideal possibility, as Utopia, his special concern.

CONTENTS

Grateful acknowledgement is made to Lewis Mumford for his fore-word. The authors also wish to thank the photographers for their excellent prints and the travel agencies of the countries represented for their valuable suggestions.

Geographical spellings follow Webster whenever possible; other main sources of reference have been the American Oxford Atlas and Baedeker. For easy cross reference, the subjects illustrated are identified in the text pages by small capitals.

INTRODUCTION

Europe, A Journey with Pictures, is a traveler's hors d'oeuvre, to whet the appetite. Also it may serve to revive memory. For photographs can do for us all what the cupcakes of Cambrai did for Marcel Proust; grant us, vicariously, an impression of the "frozen music" that is the architecture of the great cathedrals, of the strength that comes from lifting up our eyes to the eternal hills, be they Alps, Dolomites, or the Mountains of Mourne.

The purpose of this book has been to present beautiful and interesting places in Europe within ready reach of the traveler today. Some places are well known, others less well known. The photographs, taken by some of the great photographers of America and Europe, illustrate what might well be termed a romantic present-day grand tour. An attempt has been made in a very short space (for every province, every city, could fill books of its own) to represent the flavor of each country, its characteristic architecture, scenery, and people.

A book, like a place, must feed the heart and head as well as the eyes, for history is made not only of stone and bone but also of vine-terraced hillsides or green gardens or farms, of living people like the dancers in the Basque country or on the hill of Granada, of a Queen riding to parliament, of Swiss Guards or Greek Evzones, or of fishermen at Volendam or Nazaré. They, like countless others of Europe's millions, embody the customs and pageantry of the past.

The old grand tour of Europe may in a sense be said to have begun with the Crusades, for on their way to Jerusalem the knights and their followers put in a lot of (sometimes involuntary) sightseeing. In medieval times pilgrimages were grand tours indeed, whether undertaken seriously by the pious or for fun, as by such incurable gadabouts as the wife of Bath, who had been to Rome and to Saint James of Compostela. After the Reformation Bacon wrote sage advice on travel, and Sir Philip Sidney, for all his three years on the Continent, showed that not all "Englishmen Italianate" were "devils incarnate." In Lassels' *Voyage to Italy,* dated 1670, the name first occurs: "The Grand Tour of France and the Giro of Italy." During the seventeenth and eighteenth centuries a tour of Europe was even more essential to any young man of position than a university education; hundreds ventured abroad, though often no farther than Versailles and Fontainebleau! Americans went early to visit Europe; in 1776 a young Virginian found it the general habit among persons of quality no less west of the Atlantic than east.

In the present century, when travel is no longer restricted to the few possessed of much leisure and much money, wave upon wave of pleasure-bent Americans leave these shores each year in ships and planes. Their target is Europe and their ammunition is boundless energy, enthusiasm, and an eagerness to see and do everything they possibly can in the very short space of time most of them can afford. And quite naturally. For most Americans, some part of Europe is home, infinitely precious because *there* are

> The ashes of his fathers
> And the temples of his gods.

At near mid-century, the Iron Curtain removed from Europe many countries that were in the old grand tour. Geographically, the curtain dropped almost all the way along the relief division of Europe into east and west, cutting off the Central Plain east of the Bohemian Plateau and the Hungarian and Walachian plains. This book therefore contains, alas, no pictures of Bulgaria, Czechoslovakia, Estonia, Hungary, Latvia, Lithuania, Poland, Rumania, or Russia itself. Not only are satisfactory postwar photographs unavailable, but easy travel is also out of the question, for the present at least. It would only be tantalizing, not to say misleading, to show old pictures of the Hradcin, Prague's great castle; or the cupolas of Tirnova, "Little Rome" in Slovakia; or the ski slopes of

Zacopane in the Polish Carpathians; or the tower of Saints Peter and Paul in Leningrad; or sunny Varna on the Black Sea. Yet even without these parts of eastern Europe, the journey is still vast and fabulous.

Our tour considers Great Britain and Ireland first, then France, then Belgium, Holland, Denmark, Norway, Sweden, and Finland. Next Germany (west), Austria, Switzerland, Italy, Greece, Yugoslavia, and finally Spain and Portugal. Thus, mainly, it follows the clock- or sunwise journey of the New World explorer as he sets out in his quest of the Old, against the wave of history which swept humanity into Europe via the Balkans, or over the "chain of not very high mountains" as Hitler called the Urals.

In his autobiography, *This Was My World,* Robert St. John writes: "On the opposite side of the ship, so near that a man could swim, was Europe. I had no idea whether it was France, Belgium, or England, or perhaps even one of the Scandinavian coasts, but it glistened in the dawn, and seemed so clean and peaceful. This was Europe, and a child from a prairie state was looking at it with my own eyes." And it is that "with my own eyes" which is the key to Europe. For the only way to prepare to go there is to learn how and what to see. Europe, for all its treasures, is no mere museum; it is warm and living, although it might sometimes seem that the vitality is generated by tensions, and that the sum of these, temporarily canceling each other out, is that "balance of power" and marginal equilibrium which Europeans call peace.

Europe is still a wonderful continent for a vacation, whatever the hobby, sport, or interest sought. There could hardly be better music than at Salzburg, better skiing than in Norway or at Davos, better swimming than at Antibes or Capri, better eating than in France. Tennis could not be played in better conditions than at Ranelagh or Hurlingham, golf than at Saint Andrews or in Torremolinos, Spain. Fox hunting is most fun in Ireland, most splendid in the English shires. And there is winter skating along the moonlit Dutch canals; horse racing to watch at Auteuil or Ascot, and the Easter Fair at

Seville. There is sea almost everywhere for sailing, rivers and lakes for fishing; and the flea market in Paris and the open-air market in London are still the best places for a bargain. All of picturesque Europe is overnight by air, five days by boat, and can be reached for as little as $500 round trip from New York.

In spite of the climatic variations, of England's rains or Venice' drains, today's traveler, whether veritable or vicarious, needs little baggage. Traveler's checks, nylon clothing, and light luggage make everyone mobile, whether car, air, train, or sea borne. And what each country lacks in the way of small accessories—where tissues are expensive, where combs are dear—is part of the international currency of traveler's wrinkles. But what should always be brought everywhere in great abundance are questions. As T. S. Eliot says, "We know all the answers, it is the questions that we do not know." And, in face of her infinite variety, the traveler to Europe should be forever questioning. Why, for example, are national virtues, or vices, so distinct? To take a case in point, the Scottish are stingy, and so are the French; or, to put it another way (for we love them dearly), the Scots are economical, and so are the Gauls. But why do the Scottish and French forms of this virtue or vice take such totally different forms? The French will stand you all the drinks (and some more) you can take at a café, until the saucers by which the reckoning is made topple over, but will hardly ever ask you to their homes. The Scots take you home to "high tea" and kippers on first meeting, but are canny about who pays at the pub. The French hoard bits of string and buy books. The Scots deal in three-penny bits and spend more than most people on education. In France you cannot go into a church with sleeves higher than the elbow; in Scotland you still shock the local inhabitants if you play tennis or golf on a Sunday. Why? Some of the answers are history, some geography, some anthropology, some nationalism, some temperament, and some religion. And some of these questions have no answers, and these are the best of all.

ENGLAND AND WALES

England, wrote John Florio in 1591 "is the paradise of women, the purgatory of men and the hell of horses." That was in the reign of Elizabeth I. In the reign of Elizabeth II these propositions should, perhaps, be transposed. Should you arrive in England by sea, from the west, you may come first to Plymouth, sunny and southern. The harbor, from which Drake and the Pilgrims sailed, is still crowded with white sails as well as with huge steamships, for the Devon coast is a yachtsman's delight. Inland, the rust-red earth, cut with deep lanes, grows banks of tall foxgloves—white, spotted, pink, and purple—and tall bracken all summer long.

Or, if you come to Southampton, the third greatest seaport of Britain, handling some 26 million tons of shipping yearly, with docks that can berth the largest ships afloat, you land where King Canute, the Danish conqueror and ruler of Britain, taught his sycophant courtiers that "lands are ruled by a king on this throne, but the sea has no king but God alone." Crowned, sitting on the sand, he rebuked the incoming tide; when it disobeyed his orders and washed his feet, he took off his crown, placed it in Winchester Cathedral, and never wore it again.

If you arrive by air, England's tiny checkerboard fields that once were feudal strips partly reveal why this small and vulnerable country of 58,500 square miles (including Wales) can, on its own, feed only half of its 44 million people. Arriving from Europe by sea, you are also aware of England's moatedness. "Fog in the channel, continent isolated" is more than a newspaper headline. It is a geographical and psychological strength. The brief belt of water that Romans, Angles, Saxons, Danes, and Normans crossed to conquer, drowned the Spanish Armada, "diddled" Napoleon, and halted Hitler.

In the southwest heartland of England, close to each other, are three of the greatest "presentments of Englishry" ever made: Stonehenge, Wilton, and Salisbury Cathedral. STONEHENGE and Avebury are both set high on Salisbury Plain, which actually is a group of unforested downs, grassy, with wide views. Stonehenge is the most famous prehistoric monument in Europe, and is almost entirely a product of the earlier Bronze Age (1900-1400 B.C.) but may still have been in use at the time of the Roman Conquest, A.D. 43. In spite of being almost on the highroad, it is overwhelmingly impressive. A confused mass of enormous rocks, some local, some brought by water two hundred miles from Wales, some erect, some fallen (about ninety-five in all have survived), it is unmistakably the work of man offering the greatest reverence he knows to a Power, or powers, outside himself. No photograph, however good, can adequately convey the gray hugeness of the stones, many with tenons and mortises, or the desolate emptiness of the high, bare country around. Most things in England are on a small scale, the countryside is crowded and cozy; everywhere are low-ceilinged cottages, narrow roads, small shops, tiny automobiles, and neat villages. But here, in sharp contrast, is a vast uncouthness more comparable with the Sahara.

Not twenty miles away is Avebury, even older than Stonehenge, and remarkably similar with its concentric circles of long stones, and Silbury Hill, which is 170 feet high and 500 feet around at the base.

Wilton, like Beaulieu, Knole, and countless other great English country houses, was an abbey until the Reformation, when it was given to Henry VIII's brother-in-law, William Herbert, who became earl of Pembroke. The porch was designed by Hans Holbein; Inigo Jones, Vandyke, and others decorated the towers, the chambers, and the scenes; Palladio designed the theatric bridge over the river. Charles I, Aubrey tells us, "did love Wilton above all places, and came thither every summer."

Salisbury was the first great church built in England in the Pointed, or Early English, style. It is extraordinarily perfect, whether seen from afar, as in Constable's great picture, or from nearby, set on its charming green, or from within. The nave, the choir, the cloisters, and the chapter house all accord admirably together, and the close, bordered with seventeenth- and eighteenth-century houses, is delightfully sleepy. The city of Salisbury is "new," a migration, about 1220, from Old Sarum, or Sorbiodunum (the dry city). This was a Celtic town, occupied by the Romans, taken by the Saxons about 552, then by the Danes, then by William the Conqueror himself. It is chiefly famous (or infamous) because for five hundred years after it was deserted it still returned two members to Parliament!

There are around thirteen thousand villages in England, and so many are good— better—best! In the south you may find Cowdray, where Queen Elizabeth I killed four deer with her crossbow in the park; Bosham, where a little Saxon princess was found, her form still clear in the white bone dust when her coffin was opened; Lacock, serene around its abbey, or Castle Combe, which is supposed to have the best village street of any, or charming WINSFORD.

Traveling through the southwest country you should also take in Cornwall with its picturesque coastal villages like Saint Ives and Bude, and Tintagel, associated with King Arthur. Though Keats found the neighboring Devonshire climate, like Lydia Languish, to be "tearful, and her men diminutive and cowardly," Shelley wrote lyrical verses while living in Lynmouth with his wife. Southey was equally enchanted with CLOVELLY, where no two of its whitewashed houses are at the same level on the main street. Dickens, too, made Clovelly famous in his *A Message from the Sea.*

BATH is the Aquae Solis of the Romans, in whose stone baths one still can most agreeably swim in the warmest of natural spring water, all the year round. Chaucer's Wife of Bath was typical of the medieval wealth of the city. In the seventeenth century it was royal and sometimes lewd. Samuel Pepys visited it with his wife and two friends on the evening of June 12, 1668 (the King and Queen had recently visited the Baths in hopes of finding a cure for the Queen's sterility). "Up at four o'clock, being by appointment called up to the Cross bath . . . and by and by, though we designed to have done before company come, much company come, very fine ladies, and the manner pretty enough, only methinks it cannot be clean to go so many bodies together in the same water!" But Bath was transformed from "a small provincial watering place into a second Pompeii" by the genius of John Wood and his son. "The classical austerity, elegance and dignity of eighteenth century Bath has won renown among all persons of taste." Tobias Smollett further declares that "The Circus is a pretty bauble contrived for show, and looks like Vespasian's amphitheatre turned outside in." Prior Park, Ralph Allen's wonderful Palladian house, where Alexander Pope and William Pitt loved to visit, Queen Square, Royal Crescent, and other equally noted landmarks, make of Bath "A Mecca of noble Palladian architecture." One of the few bridges of its kind is the covered PULTENEY BRIDGE, built by Robert Adam in 1770 and containing shops. The bridge was visited by Jane Austen who, like Smollett and Sheridan, wrote in, and of, this enchanting city.

In Hampshire, Beaulieu, lovely as its name, is on the edge of the New Forest, at the head of a creek of Southampton Water. The pretty thatch-roofed, timbered and whitewashed cottages and inns like THE CAT AND THE FIDDLE which flourishes at Hinton Admiral are typical of this county, and of neighboring Surrey. Both counties also share heaths of gorse and heather. The purple vistas fringed with pine woods around Hindhead, where Conan Doyle wrote *The Hound of the Baskervilles,* James Barrie *Peter Pan,* and where Bernard Shaw once had a house, make walking a joy.

The south coast is studded, all the way from Margate in Kent to Lyme Regis in Dorset, with resorts beloved of honeymooners, children with nannies, and trippers of every kind, size, and shape. These seaside towns and villages, whether old established and large, like Eastbourne or Bognor Regis, or tiny, like Angmering, often have been described, with their attractive flower gardens, piers, bands, sands, and unrationed sun. One of their great admirers was Rudyard Kipling, among whose most-quoted lines are:

> Each to his choice, and I rejoice
> The lot has fallen to me,
> In a fair land, yea a fair land,
> Yea, Sussex by the sea.

Rivaled only by the cliffs at Dover are the WHITE CLIFFS called the Seven Sisters, undulating at the end of the South Downs, near Eastbourne. The White Cliffs and Dover itself, where Julius Caesar is thought to have landed, have inspired many poets, and how variously! Shakespeare's

> . . . how fearful
> And dizzy 'tis to cast one's eye so low!
> The crows and choughs that wing the midway air
> Show scarce so gross as beetles: half way down
> Hangs one that gathers samphire; dreadful trade!
> Methinks he seems no bigger than his head.
> The fishermen that walk upon the beach
> Appear like mice; . . .
> I'll look no more,
> Lest my brain turn and the deficient sight
> Topple down headlong.
>
> (from *King Lear*)

is a long way from Alice Duer Miller's sentimental *The White Cliffs,* or Matthew Arnold's

> . . . the cliffs of England stand
> Glimmering and vast, out in the tranquil bay.

Picturesque Rye, with the cobbled streets walked by Henry James, and lovely Winchelsea are two more of the old Cinque Ports. East of Brighton is Lewes, where Simon de Montfort, with the insurgent barons, won his great victory over Henry III. Henry's son, Prince Edward, might have won the day but lost it chasing the Londoners, against whom he had a special grudge because they had "insulted the Queen his mother on her way by water from the Tower to Windsor by throwing stones and dirt at her."

Lewes is near Glyndebourne, where the music festival takes place each year. The opera house is set in the loveliest of gardens. Evening dress is obligatory, and the self-conscious music fans, tiaraed and bejeweled, crowd the commuters taking the 5:05 from London's Victoria Station, but look delicious in this country setting. Near Lewes is charming Alfriston, which has a real spreading chestnut tree to mark the village center.

Of the great castles in the south, HURST-MONCEAUX, built in 1440 and lavishly restored, is one of the last and most impressive of the fortified houses. Windows, door cases, coping and water tables are of stone, but Horace Walpole could describe it in his time as having remained "in its native brickhood, without the luxury of whitewash." Pevensey Bay is five miles away, where William the Conqueror landed with 900 ships and 60,000 men, including horsemen. Bodiam, licensed as a castle in the Hundred Years War against France "for resistance against our enemies" was built in 1383, three years after the French had burned Rye, Winchelsea, and Hastings. Hever Castle, where Anne Boleyn was born, is full of relics of the "brown girl with a wen and an extra finger" for whom Henry VIII left his Catherine and the Catholic Church. And Penshurst Place, near the pleasant old watering place Tunbridge Wells, is where Sir Philip Sidney and his brothers and sisters grew up. Philip, who died of a wound at thirty-two, trod "from the cradle to the grave, amidst incense and flowers, and died in a dream of glory." He was, for all time, the incarnation of what the average Englishman means when he talks about a gentleman. Penshurst, a mixture of castle and mansion, with towers, courts and high halls, and with both formal and informal gardens, fountains, and a heronry, is as it was in Philip Sidney's day, and still belongs to his family.

KNOLE, perhaps the most famous of all English houses, with its 365 rooms, 52 staircases, and 7 courtyards, is neighbor to Penshurst. Many authors have written of Knole, but perhaps Virginia Woolf best described those five acres of rose-colored brick: "By short cuts known to him, he made his way now through the vast congeries of rooms and staircases to the banqueting hall, five acres distant on the other side of the house. . . . It looked a town rather than a house . . .

Courts and buildings grey, red, plum color, lay orderly and symmetrical. The courts were some of them oblong and some square; in this was a fountain; in that a statue; the buildings were some of them low, some pointed; here was a chapel, there a belfry; spaces of the greenest grass lay in between and clumps of cedar trees and beds of bright flowers; all were clasped—yet so well set out was it that it seemed that every part had room to spread itself fittingly . . . This vast, yet ordered building which could house a thousand men and perhaps two thousand horses was built, Orlando thought, by workmen whose names were unknown."

Almost every great house and castle in England can be viewed by anyone today and not expensively. And every square mile of the country has at least one lovely "place." Some are famous for their settings, as Bibury in Gloucestershire, or Arundel Castle, or Alnwick in Northumberland. Others for their architecture, as Compton Wynyates in Warwickshire or Blickling in Norfolk; others for the treasures they contain, such as the Queen's own Windsor and Castle Howard; others for their size, antiquity, ghosts, or gardens. They come in every shape and age. —some, and of the loveliest, are only one room through; others, like Vanbrugh's Blenheim, are, as the English say, "plain bloated."

The small towns of England are at least as attractive as the villages. Arundel, steeply clinging to its high hill, is almost Umbrian the way it starts out of its watery plain. And it is splendidly feudal. The Duke of Norfolk, Hereditary Earl Marshal, who arranges coronations, royal funerals and the like, is Earl of Arundel.

> Since William rose and Harold fell
> There have been counts of Arundel,
> And Earls old Arundel shall have
> While rivers flow and forests wave.

Nearby is Goodwood, where the Duke of Richmond lives, a descendant of Charles II's Nell Gwyn. Steyning and Burwash have great charm. Brighton, with its Regency crescents and squares and its sublimely absurd pavilion, and Chichester, like Winchester a Roman town, are each in their very different ways, delightful. Mayfield, on a ridge at the edge of Ashdown Forest, has an old palace of the archbishops of Canterbury which is now a convent.

Since 597, when Saint Augustine came to CANTERBURY at the direction of Saint Gregory the Great, that city has been the metropolitan see of all England. Many of the memorials of Saint Thomas à Becket's murder are still visible in the chapel or transept of the martyrdom. Here, too, the Black Prince is buried, and Stephen Langton, who was archbishop at the time of the Magna Carta.

In medieval times pilgrims came from all over the known world to Canterbury; only Rome, Jerusalem and Compostela rivaled it. Henry VIII made offerings at the shrine in 1520, and eighteen years later he ordered it plundered and "the holy blisful martyr" Becket's bones burned. Erasmus, who visited the Cathedral in 1513, wrote "the least valuable portion was gold. Every part glistened, shone, and sparkled with rare and very large jewels, some of them exceeding the size of a goose's egg." In a vault at Saint Dunstan's is the head of Sir Thomas More, hid there by Margaret Roper after it had been exposed on London Bridge for fourteen days. It will be remembered that David Copperfield and his aunt went to Mr. Wickfield's house in Canterbury, "a very old house bulging out over the road, a house with long, low lattice windows bulging out still farther, and beams with carved heads on the ends bulging out too, so that I fancied the whole house was leaning forward, trying to see who was passing on the pavement below." Canterbury is full of recollections of great men: Christopher Marlowe, "with mouth of gold, and morning in his eyes," was born here. When Queen Elizabeth I came, she was "exceeding magnifical," and asked Archbishop Parker's wife

> Madam I cannot,
> Mistress I would not,
> Woman, what am I to call thee?

Today, the Church of England Festival, for which such famous authors as T. S. Eliot, Christopher Fry, and Dorothy Sayers have written plays, is held in Canterbury, and so is the long-drawn-out Cricket Week.)

("Who is tired of London," Dr. Johnson remarked, "is tired of life." But where, in LONDON, does one begin?) By air one arrives near the Great West Road and the undistinguished ordinariness of Kensington High Street, landing, it is true, in Victoria. By train, Waterloo or Victoria are more satisfactory. Crossing Waterloo, or better Westminster, Bridge there is Wordsworth's greatest sonnet:

> Earth has not anything to show more fair:
> Dull would he be of soul who could pass by
> A sight so touching in its majesty:
> This city now doth like a garment wear
> The beauty of the morning: silent, bare,
> Ships, towers, domes, theatres, and temples
>   lie
> Open unto the fields, and to the sky,—
> All bright and glittering in the smokeless
>   air . . .

which is hard today to reconcile with the noise and belching smoke of the gasworks on the river's bank, or with the urbane London County Council building across the river from (the HOUSES OF PARLIAMENT, Built by Sir Charles Barry between 1840-1860, the Houses are pure Victorian neo-Gothic; yet for some reason they are not at all commonplace, like the Law Courts, nor monstrous, like the Albert Memorial. The chimes of BIG BEN are magnificent. So close together are Westminster Abbey, Westminster School, Buckingham Palace, the Cenotaph, Whitehall, and tiny Downing Street that no mile in England is as crowded with dignity or history. The heart of London is right there where Francis Thompson, the self-styled "bum," saw

> the traffic of Jacob's ladder
> pitched between heaven and Charing Cross.

(Westminster Abbey looks its best for royalty: a coronation or even a royal funeral becomes it vastly. At other times it seems too haphazard and disorganized, though the lovely Henry VII chapel makes an exquisite setting for weddings, and the Poets' Corner is an institution, and must be saluted as such. Just behind Westminster School is the en-

chanting little baroque church known as Queen Anne's footstool—tradition is that the Queen kicked her footstool across the room in disgust at her architect and said, "go copy that." On Grosvenor Road is the Tate Gallery, with French Impressionist pictures, English moderns, and a most delightful restaurant decorated by the late Rex Whistler.

(Trafalgar Square, at the top of Whitehall, is the popular, as Westminster is the political, center of the British Empire. Here is King Charles I's superb statue:

> Comely and calm, he rides
> Hard by his own Whitehall.
> Only the night wind glides;
> No crowds, nor rebels, brawl.

Here is Nelson's column, with the gentle lions; here too is the National Gallery with its wonderful collection of old masters, and tapestries (described by a Cockney to his son as "what they 'ad before they 'ad wallpapers"). Here too is Saint Martins-in-the-Fields, which is open all night for the homeless and is as famous for Tubby Clayton, the "Toc H" chaplain of World War I who popularized it, as for its Wren steeple.

(The West End is London's fashionable shopping center, with Bond Street, Oxford Street, Regent Street, Grosvenor Square, and Piccadilly Circus (where the bobbies are as much a part of the scene as the statues of Eros). Near here is Soho, and Shaftesbury Avenue with its belt of theaters. A visit to Covent Garden for opera and ballet, and an evening with Shakespeare across the river at the Old Vic are on most people's lists of things to do. So is a browse down Charing Cross Road with its secondhand bookshops.

All around Charing Cross many buildings disappeared during the last war. Saint Clement Danes still stands, but one of the loveliest of the Wren churches, Saint Bride's, was completely destroyed. The Temple Church, too, was hit, and the charming Inns of Court—Gray's Inn, Lincoln's Inn, and the Inner Temple—were all variously damaged, though their scars show less and less. SAINT PAUL'S on the whole rather profited, for it stands out more dramatically than it ever did, with the broader space around it.

17

The Tower of London is more sinister, perhaps, than any other famous historical building in the world. It is associated only with dismal disgrace, with tragedy at every level, from the time of William the Conqueror, who built the Norman Keep to overawe early Londoners, until that of Sir Roger Casement, who was hanged there in the first World War. It has housed numberless prisoners—royal, gentle and simple—and few indeed escaped. Here is "Little Ease," a hole where the prisoner could neither stand nor sit nor lie, and here are the very racks and thumbscrews used until the time of James I. Here is the Traitor's Gate, with its 61-foot keystoneless span, through which Queens Anne Boleyn, Catherine Howard, and Elizabeth I entered, as did Sir Thomas More, the archbishops Cranmer and Laud, the earls of Essex and of Strafford, the Duke of Monmouth, and many others. In the Bloody Tower, Sir Walter Raleigh spent thirteen years, and Sir John Eliot died here of the cold. One of the worst murders committed in the Bloody Tower was, of course, that of the Little Princes: King Edward V, aged twelve, and his brother, the Duke of York. In the Wakefield Tower the saintly founder of Eton College and Kings College, Cambridge, King Henry VI, was murdered. Now the Crown Jewels are kept there. Except for the Black Prince's ruby worn in the front of the State Crown, few are really old. The Crown Jewels and plate were all "popped" in the Civil War, first by King Charles I, then those that remained by the Parliament. At the Commonwealth auction, the Black Prince's ruby sold for £4, the agate chalice of Edward the Confessor (listed as a "large glass cup") for £102.5, Queen Edith's crown for £16, and "one pair of buskins, cloth of silver, and silver stockings, very old," for 2 shillings and 6 pence.

Every night curfew rings at sunset, and every night the Ceremony of the Keys takes place at the Tower, ending with the words "Advance, Queen Elizabeth's Keys, all's well." All seems very well to the English in their second Elizabethan age. That radiantly beautiful young woman, Her Majesty Queen Elizabeth II, happily and suitably married, with a son to succeed her ("Of course we knew she'd have a boy—Elizabeth has never let us down," her relatives said when Prince Charles was born), is the very spirit of England incarnate, and is much the loveliest of all the sights of London. Rarely has anyone in history so looked his part, or so obviously enjoyed playing it; and to all members of the British Commonwealth of Nations their "regular, royal Queen" is the very bond of their unity.

Some of London's other best sights are vistas—of the Foreign Office from the bridge in Saint James's Park, of the fountains at the end of Kensington Gardens, of London from Highgate or the river from Cheyne Walk. Indeed, many of the best things in London are outside the center, like Kew Gardens, Hampton Court, Richmond Park, and Hampstead Heath *not* on a holiday.

Windsor Castle is as romantic as the Tower of London is tragic. Here James I of Scotland looked from his prison window and saw *It is the queen's palace near London.*

> walking 'neath my prison tower
> Full secretly, new coming here to prayer,
> The fairest and the freshest young flower
> That ever I beheld before that hour.
> Entranced I gazed, and with the sudden start
> Rushed instant all my blood into my heart.

Queen Elizabeth II brought her young husband here when both were made Knights of the Garter by her father in Saint George's Chapel. Here in the library is the great collection of Leonardo da Vinci drawings, and the Castle with its unique skyline dominates the steep little town of the *Merry Wives* and even enters into the life of Eton down below. Eton is 1440 brick, and wonderfully beautiful; certainly by any Platonic standards boys raised in surroundings so architecturally admirable *should* be civilized. The playing fields—on which the battle of Waterloo was supposedly won—seem strangely small. Eton should be seen on one of its feast days, when matches are being played, or on the "Glorious Fourth" of June when the torchlight procession of boats, their crews standing with oars aloft, passes unsteadily through the summer twilight to the sound of music and

18 *the 3 main universities of England are almost as old as they are famous.*

an occasional plop when a participant falls in. Also west of London are the pleasant small watery towns in the Thames Valley—Henley, where the regatta is held, Maidenhead, and High Wycombe. West Wycombe, with eighteenth-century stone "follies" on its green hills, is a delightful village, and Medmenham, where the Georgian rakes had themselves such a time, looks pious and pretty today "with weeping willows on the fringe of the abbey lawn bending gracefully over the water like a row of maidens washing their hair in the clear stream."

OXFORD, the suburb of Cowley as it has ribaldly been called, is probably, after Florence, the most overwritten city in the world. Like Florence, too, it is no backwater. So crowded today that it is often almost impossible to walk on its pavements, it is at once the city where Morris automobiles are made, a busy county seat, and the "Beautiful city" of Matthew Arnold.

O ye spires of Oxford! domes and towers!
Gardens and groves! your presence over-
        powers
The soberness of reason.

How wrong he was! The Oxford Movement of the nineteenth century was at least as important as any other spiritual or political movement; and today the man who proved by doing it, that an airplane could be got out of a spin—Lord Cherwell—is an Oxford don, as is a recent British ambassador to Washington, Sir Oliver Franks. Indeed, Oxford dons seem constantly to be borrowed to run the British Empire.

Nearly thirty colleges, founded from the twelfth to the twentieth centuries, house the three thousand male, and close to two thousand female, Oxford students. The four greatest colleges—Christ Church, founded by Cardinal Wolsey; Magdalen, with its TOWER and bridge; New College; and Balliol, as ugly as the others are beautiful—have wonderful gardens, lawns, and walks around them. Asked how they acquired such good lawns, Goldwin Smith replied, "It's the simplest thing in the world; just roll and mow regularly for four hundred years." The public buildings, the Schools, the Radcliffe Cam-

era, the Bodleian Library, the Ashmolean Museum (where the Alfred Jewel is kept), the Sheldonian Theatre (built by Sir Christopher Wren), Saint Mary the Virgin—the pre-Reformation University Chapel, where Amy Robsart was buried and Latimer and Ridley were tried and Newman preached Sunday after Sunday—all are unique and infinitely moving.

Nowhere are so many styles and periods so happily combined as in Oxford. Merton has a lovely statue of Saint John the Baptist; Corpus Christi, a cylindrical sundial; Trinity, trellised walks of pollard limes; Queens, designed by Wren, its almost Dutch orderliness and its seventeenth-century glass. Each college is unique, and in each history is harmony. No city in the world—not Florence, Salzburg, Paris, nor Rome—combines stones and bones, ghosts and gardens, more successfully.

The Martyrs' Memorial at Oxford commemorates three Cambridge men, and CAMBRIDGE, supposedly founded by a mythical Spanish king called Cantaber, became a university in 1209 when a body of scholars migrated from Oxford and established themselves "in that distant marsh town." In 1318 Pope John XXII recognized it as a university and to Cambridge Elizabeth I granted a charter in 1573, and set Lord Burleigh as Chancellor over it. Cambridge is wholly a university town, like Coimbra in Portugal or Princeton in the United States—and unlike Oxford! Trinity College, founded by Henry VIII, was rebuilt in the reign of James I by the Master, Thomas Neville, who "never had his like for a splendid courageous and bountiful gentleman." Isaac Barrow, master of Trinity in 1669, resigned the professorship of mathematics in favor of Isaac Newton, and Richard Bentley, master in 1700, built an observatory in Trinity. Since then Cambridge has excelled in science, Oxford in letters. Trinity Court, slightly larger than Tom Quad, has a charming fountain instead of Tom's shallow pool. The Christopher Wren Library is paneled by Grinling Gibbons, and the West Gateway, leading to the lime avenue, has a view over the river Cam.

Among the well-known Cambridge men are Cromwell, Darwin, Wordsworth; among the colleges are Queens, Jesus, Peterhouse (the first to be founded), Christ's, King's, and Saint John's College, founded in 1511, with its famous BRIDGE OF SIGHS over the "Backs." The College Chapel at King's is one of the most perfect buildings in the world. Built between 1446 and 1515, it has twenty-five stained-glass windows dating from 1515, and all the ancillary details, as well as the wonderful singing there by the King's College Choir, are flawless. Indeed, it is almost too much, and the visitor retires to the Backs (the lawns, gardens, and groves behind the colleges) with a sigh of surfeit. As Wordsworth put it:

> . . . Give all thou canst. High Heaven rejects the lore
> Of nicely calculated less or more:
> So deem'd the man who fashion'd for the sense
> These lofty pillars, spread that branching roof
> Self-poised, and scoop'd into ten thousand cells
> Where light and shade repose, where music dwells
> Lingering—and wandering on as loath to die.

Perhaps one can safely say that Oxford is the more beautiful town, Cambridge much the more beautiful university.

The Cotswold hills contain some of the most enchanting villages and small towns in England. Minster Lovell; Burford, lolloping down its hill, every house different, and each a gem; Cirencester and Lechlade; Fairford, with medieval windows unmatched even by the Seven Sisters at York; Bibury, with Arlington Row; and Eastleach, with two churches for good measure on one green; Painswick, with its pride of great yew trees in the churchyard; Broadway and Edge, Chipping Campden and Cleeve Hill. Northleach has a glorious spire, and Bourton on the Water has a river meandering through the streets; at Hatherop the Coln was curled to please the castle's owner. It is hard to find lovelier valleys anywhere than those of the Coln, the Windrush, and the Evenlode, all tributaries of the Thames.

Northwest is STRATFORD ON AVON, a one-man town as no other in the world, except perhaps Weimar. Here Shakespeare was born, on April 23—so suitably on Saint George's Day—1564, and here he died, on his birthday, in 1616. Here, in Holy Trinity Church, at the end of a lime avenue, he is buried. The great perpendicular east window lights the poet's monument—a colored bust, probably from a death mask, in a Jacobean niche. Below are slabs covering Shakespeare's body, his wife, and that of his favorite daughter, Anne Hall. On his slab is written:

> Good friend, for Jesus' sake forbeare
> To dig the dust encloased here;
> Blessed be the man that spares these stones
> And curst be he that moves my bones.

The Shakespeare Memorial Theatre, in excellent taste, is always crowded during the summer-long season. And everyone visits ANNE HATHAWAY'S COTTAGE and sees the typically English, well-kept garden. Not far from Stratford is SULGRAVE MANOR, the handsome stone house of George Washington's ancestors, with portraits of America's first president (by Gilbert Stuart) and of his forebears. The house was bought from Henry VIII in 1539 by Laurence Washington, twice mayor of Northampton, and has both the royal arms of the Tudors and those of the Washingtons on its walls. Following Shakespeare's Avon west toward Arden, the river leaves Warwickshire, one of the great hunting counties, and parallels Gloucestershire.

Within a forty-mile radius of Stratford many great battles were fought—Worcester, Tewkesbury, Bosworth, Naseby. It was of Naseby that Macaulay wrote one of his most famous lays, telling how "Astley, and Sir Marmaduke, and Rupert of the Rhine" were beaten by the Parliament, and how Charles I fled the field. He spent the night at Wistow, leaving his saddle behind him. Worcester and Gloucester have lovely cathedrals, Evesham a lovely bell tower, and Tewkesbury a fine abbey.

South, beyond the Severn Tunnel, are the Welsh Marches; whereon is Caerleon upon Usk. Chepstow Castle, en route to Tintern, and Symond's Yat, above Monmouth, are both romantic pauses up the beautiful river Wye. The view from the top of the Wyncliff, nine hundred feet above the river, is one of the most famous river scenes in Europe. Paths lead through the woods to Tintern Abbey, founded in 1131 by the Cistercians. The roof is gone, but the main walls are standing and give an idea of its former majesty, set in solemn, splendid scenery. Herefordshire is to the north, while Shropshire, also bordering Wales, is soaked in Housman's delicate melancholy; only the grave is, as he suggests, a "quieter place than Clun," and

> On Wenlock Edge the wood's in trouble;
> His forest fleece the Wrekin heaves;
> The gale, it plies the saplings double,
> And thick on Severn snow the leaves.
> T'would blow like this through holt and
>   hanger
> When Uricon the city stood . . .

Uricon (now Wroxeter), five miles from Shrewsbury, was a city bigger than Pompeii, the last stronghold of Rome against the Britons in Wales. The garrison was murdered to the last man when the Romans withdrew. Shrewsbury is almost moated by the Severn and is full of good houses, has a fine castle and a Royal Free Grammar School where Sir Philip Sidney and butcher Judge Jeffreys both went to school. LUDLOW, another delightful border town, is where Milton wrote *Comus* for the two sons of the Earl of Bridgewater who, with the original of the Lady, had been lost overnight in Hay Wood. *Comus* was first performed in the castle grounds in 1634, when Milton was twenty-five, and again, delightfully, in the same place for the third centenary in 1934.

Wales is curiously different from England. A pall of cloud often hangs over it, and the mountains, not high but real and remote, are quietly somber and nostalgic. From Abergavenny one reaches the heart of them quickly, but still today many of the valleys can be entered only on foot. On the Monmouthshire border, which is really neither quite Wales nor England, is Llanthony, a twelfth-century abbey, in ruins, and now a most agreeable inn. Anglers can catch their trout and eat them for breakfast in the old prior's house which belonged once to Walter Savage Landor, the poet. The mountain village of Capel-y-Ffin is below one of the oldest chapels in Great Britain, tiny, and now deserted, alone among the larks and grazing sheep. Radnor has a forest and a castle, and all the Black Mountains are tremendously dramatic, empty and aloof, with huge, hideous, infinitely dreary mining towns in their valleys—Aberdare, Merthyr Tydfil, Brynmawr; and beyond them the high Carmarthenshire and Cardiganshire hills. Saint David's, the archiepiscopal see of Wales, is a charming little town with a cathedral built in 1176, a bird sanctuary island nearby, and always hills, and more hills. Aberystwyth is a coastal resort, and among the best places to stay for seeing Wales are Dolgelley, at the foot of Cader Idris, and Llangollen. The latter is near Valle Crucis, a ruin almost as perfect as Tintern or Fountains.

LLANGOLLEN is the meeting place for the annual Eisteddfod, a "sing-fest" of Welsh and international competing choirs. Llangollen is also famous for its eighteenth-century blue stockings, the two Irish "Ladies," sworn to celibacy, who lived in PLAS NEWYDD, the splendid old timbered house surrounded by a garden of clipped yew trees. Their faithful servant bought the house with her savings and deeded it to them!

CONWAY CASTLE, built by Edward I in 1284, is within its perfect feudal *enceinte,* whose walls are strengthened by twenty-one towers. Caernarvon is the other big Edward I castle, from which his son was proclaimed Prince of Wales.

Chester, quaint and old, just east of the Welsh border, is particularly remembered for its Roman remains, half-timbered houses, and streets lined with unique "rows," or two-storied arcades, where the townsfolk do their shopping. From Chester Gladstone's Hawarden, exactly as he left it, can be reached.

The poets' Lake District, a small area but full of picturesque and lovely landscapes, with its walks and climbs and its memories of Coleridge and Wordsworth, lies north of industrial Lancashire toward the Scottish border. Derwentwater, eulogized by Ruskin and lived near by Hugh Walpole, is the broadest of the lakes and the most popular. North of the beautiful Lake District is the great sweep of the Scottish border, as different from the Welsh as it is from the Midlands or the South Downs. Here are the moors and the dales, with cloud patterns constantly changing them. The country is on a grand scale, and the high fells give the land an open, august feeling. Traveling northeast, in Northumberland, we find the sites of the great battles against the Scots: Otterburn and Flodden (a mile from Branxton). Here, too, are the sea castles, like Bamburgh and Dunstanburgh, and the ones inland, like Alnwick, Ford, Chillingham (which has the only herd of wild cattle in England), and Hexham. The Roman Wall of Hadrian, built against the wild Scots, is still visible for most of its original extent.

(On the southern border of the county is Newcastle, with its coal industry, and farther below, Durham with the enormous cathedral which vies in size and fame with York Minster. Built in the late eleventh century, Durham is the sturdiest Norman building in England.) Here Saint Cuthbert and Saint Bede the Venerable are buried; the castle and indeed the whole town, islanded on three sides by the river Wear, are massively solid, as is Barnard Castle to the southwest.

(Yorkshire, England's largest county, is also the Brontë country, immortalized by the genius of the sisters, Charlotte, Emily, and Anne, brooding in their grim Haworth parsonage. Here are the moors, wild as Heathcliffe, here are industrial towns like Sheffield, Leeds, and Huddersfield, and here are farming and market gardening on a large scale.) Above York and west of the north moors is RICHMOND, a gem by the rocky, rushing Swale. The large historic castle there has a perfect hundred-foot-high keep and complete walls; the prettily situated Grammar School, rebuilt in 1850, was founded by Elizabeth I. Within easy motoring distance is Easby Abbey, ruined, but with the granary preserved, Ripon, and Fountains Abbey, the most complete of all the Cistercian abbey ruins in England. On the coast is Scarborough, the large summer resort, and

Whitby where Saint Hilda founded her great abbey in 657. Within reach of the town are a wealth of castles, ruins, and country seats.

The East Coast, from Lincolnshire down to Essex, is a country of fens, or marshes drained by dikes and canals, and broads, or flat estuary-lakes. It is a farmland country of small villages with large churches, of wonderful carillons and bell ringers, of fields of flowering bulbs rivaling Holland's in springtime; of sailing boats on the "broads" in summer. Lincoln, on a ridge overlooking the fens, has a magnificent cathedral founded in the eleventh century. And Southwell Cathedral whose see, in Nottinghamshire, was founded in 627 by Paulinus, is second only to Durham as a perfect example of Norman architecture. Another great English cathedral is Ely, on the island "fortress of the fens," where Hereward the Wake played hide-and-seek with William the Conqueror.

A pleasant music floats along the mere
From monks in Ely chanting service high.
(Wordsworth)

The flat eastern counties have tremendous skyscapes, and the painters, as those of the Norwich School, for example John Sell Cotman and Old Crome, have celebrated the luminous quality of the landscape. "It has colors of its own, and its level distances know moods as various and as definitely, if not as violently, in contrast as those of the mountainous regions," writes Ronald Carton. "The meadows, green and brown and golden, pick out a diverse colored patchwork where they stretch across the shire. The woods, so green a mile away, fade into a nebulous blue-grey at greater distances. . . ."

Norfolk, Suffolk, and Essex are counties of wonderful brick houses—Gifford, and Blickling, Lord Lothian's place at Aylsham, now open as a youth hostel, being among the largest and most superb. They also contain some of the best, most unspoiled villages in England. Essex, in spite of its nearness to London, is particularly blessed and FINCHINGFIELD, according to that authority, Humphrey Pakington, is the queen of the county. "It is better to approach Finchingfield from the west or south—from the direction of Saffron Walden or of Dunmow—for you may see then with what noble sweeps the roads fall into the cup of the village green, and how they are gathered into one to pass over the little brick bridge and so up the winding street of the village." Or approach it when the MORRIS DANCERS make it festive, all dressed up in white costumes with colorful ribbons.

Colchester has a castle on the site where the ill-fated British Queen, Boadicea, outraged by Nero, and with streaming hair and clanking armor, led a widespread revolt in the first century. Near Colchester are the old Norman settlements like Layer de la Haye and Layer Marney, with its magnificent mansion built shortly after Hampton Court, and by the same architect. The little villages like Messing and Mucking are far, far prettier than they sound and Tiptree is where the best jams in England are made. All around here, as in the famous English shires, there is good FOX HUNTING, as well as point-to-point races and beagling.

To the continental European, the natives of the British Isles are completely incomprehensible. Count Keyserling found that, although the British are the least developed intellectually of all European peoples, they are the most developed psychologically. "The Englishman has, to a greater extent than any other European, an immediate contact with what there is human in man. He sees and senses first in a man that which is human. And always he recognizes, as a human right, the individual character. He never gives the impression that any 'thing' could have a greater value for him than people.' The English are the politest people in the world, perhaps partly because they are forced to live in such close contiguity, sardinewise; that silence, reserve, and respect for "otherness" are virtues beyond price. To say of someone that he is a *good quiet man* is high praise, and so, at another social level, is "she keeps herself to herself." This crowd courtesy requires, indeed maintains, the caste, or class system. A good butler would be as horrified at his master's questioning him, in however friendly a fashion, about his private life as vice versa.

SCOTLAND

In spite of the smothering, leveling niceties of B.B.C. language, distinctions remain. A Cockney still speaks differently from a Liverpudlian, a Highlander from a Glaswegian. And the difference, not only in language or accent but also in almost every other way, between the English and the Scots is extraordinary. This in spite of feuding and marrying since the beginning of time. Even during the worst of the war and postwar rationing, there was always more, and always better, food in Scotland than in England. But the raw cold there is such (except on the Gulf Stream–warmed west coast) that few English or Americans, let alone Europeans, dare or care to go to Scotland between October and April. It is as true as most generalizations that the best scenery in Scotland (which occupies 30,405 square miles) is in the west, the best buildings are in the east.

The Romans made no conquests north of the great wall. Christianity, on the other hand, came much earlier to Scotland than to England. The Candida Casa of Saint Ninian, was built about 435; its site can be seen at Whithorn near Wigtown; Glasgow was established as an episcopal see in 560 by Saint Kentigern, and Saint Columba landed in Iona in 563. These three saints came from Ireland, and the interpenetration of the two islands still goes on. Northern Ireland is largely populated by people of Scottish extraction, while Glasgow, the second city of Great Britain, includes a large element of Irish.

The Scottish Border Country is as southern in mood as Northumberland is northern. It has luxuriant vegetation; deep, leafy glens; verdant fields; and is as different as can be from the high, bare English fells and dales. The Tweed, with its superlative fishing, flows through Melrose, whose Abbey is considered "indisputably the finest ruin in Scotland." Founded by Cistercians from Rievaulx, it has lovely windows, and a gloriously rich choir loft, with slender shafts. In the ruins of Dryburgh Abbey, founded about 1100, Sir Walter Scott and his family (including John

23

Lockhart, his son-in-law and biographer) and also Earl Haig are buried. Abbotsford, Scott's home, architecturally depressing, can be seen any weekday. At Jedburgh there is a late Romanesque abbey ruin, and another, smaller one, is at Kelso. Near Hawick is *Lay of the Last Minstrel* country, and Hassendean is the home of Jock o' Hazeldean. The Eildon Hills abound in legends and are prettily shaped; at Harden, Lord Polwarth's place, is a natural enclosure into which the Scots of early days would drive the sheep they had looted from the English.

At North Berwick are the second most famous golf links in the world, the four courses of Saint Andrews being the first. Golf was played in Scotland very early—James I (whose memory haunts the nearby Bass Rock as well as Tantallon Castle, described in Scott's *Marmion*) forbade young men to play golf until they had done their archery practice. The Border Country is gay and gallant, sung by Scott, while Ayrshire was vernaculared by Robert Burns.

EDINBURGH, "above the crags that fade and gloom," as W. E. Henley wrote, is a capital as splendid as any in the world. "The Northern Athens" is set on Castle Hill and its surrounding ridges and hollows. Princes Street has often been called the finest single street in Europe, and EDINBURGH CASTLE is tremendously effective, surrounded on three sides by almost perpendicular precipices. On special occasions up here, Highlanders' kilts swirl to the skirl of bagpipes as they perform neat SWORD DANCES and flings. The Scottish National War Memorial, designed by Sir Robert Lorimer, has wonderful modern stained-glass windows by Douglas Strachan. Saint Giles' Cathedral is disappointing, but nearby HOLYROOD PALACE is full of the drama of Mary Stuart's life. It was here that her lover Rizzio was murdered. Today, at the palace, Scottish girls make their curtsy to Queen Elizabeth II. Falkland Palace, too, recalls Mary, but Mary in her happier days, and Stirling Castle, where as an infant she was crowned. Two and a half miles from Stirling, Robert Bruce, who "hobnobbed" with the spider, defeated the English at Bannockburn.

The gateway to the HIGHLANDS is Glasgow, and some of the grandest scenery in the world is near the big city. To drive over Rest-and-Be-Thankful down on to Loch Fyne, or up Glen Aray to Loch Awe, and over the Pass of Melfort to Oban, or to take a steamer along the Sound of Mull to Tobermory, in whose harbor many of the Armada ships sank, to land at Staffa and see Fingal's Cave, and at Iona, the blessed isle, is to enjoy within a small radius a combination of natural beauty and historical association hardly equaled elsewhere in Europe. Castles and abbeys, each with a story as long as the mouse's tale in *Alice,* crowd every rock and hill and glen. LOCH KATRINE and ELLEN'S ISLE, featured in Sir Walter Scott's *Lady of the Lake;* Loch Lomond, Ben Nevis; LOCH OICH which the Caledonian Canal links with LOCH NESS, famed for its mysterious monster; Oban, with its fuchsia-filled gardens and Highland Gathering; Skye, with the "far Cuchullins" that offer the "finest and most dangerous rock-climbing in Britain" and Dunvegan Castle, the oldest inhabited castle in Great Britain, where Dr. Johnson and Boswell stayed; the remote Gaelic-speaking islands in the northern seas

> Where grow no trees,
> They're called the Hebrides,

all are of the stuff that dreams are made of. At GLENFINNAN, the statue of BONNIE PRINCE CHARLIE commemorates the young Stuart claimant to the British throne who "danced with the ladies at Holyroodhouse while the British fought him at Edinburgh Castle" and who finally lost at Culloden in 1746. Deeply graven in Scottish hearts, his memory is sung in many a song:

> Will ye nae come back again,
>   Will ye nae come back again—
> Better loved ye ne'er can be—
>   Will ye nae come back again?

"That man is little to be envied," Dr. Johnson said sternly, "whose piety would not grow warmer in the ruins of Iona." The tiny island of IONA, three miles long and one wide, contains the remains of an Augustinian nunnery, Saint Oran's twelfth-century chapel, and a cemetery with the tombs of Scottish and Irish kings, including Macbeth and Duncan.

> The bell invites me.
> Hear it not, Duncan; for it is a knell
> That summons thee to heaven or to hell.

The Cathedral of Saint Mary dates from 1204, and there is also Saint Columba's stone pillar, and Saint Martin's and Maclean's Crosses, the only survivors of the 360 the island once boasted. The delightful spouting cave and Dun-I, the little flower-carpeted mountain in the middle of the island, and the Bay of the Coracle, where Saint Columba landed, are all exquisite; only Assisi in all the world keeps and conveys so completely the flavor of its saint.

Aberdeen, the city of granite that exports jokes about itself, is impressive architecturally and educationally, having an old and famous university and excellent schools. Impressive, too, is the mile-long Forth Bridge at Edinburgh, with two main 1700-foot spans. This and the Finnan viaduct of twenty-one arches (a quarter of a mile long and one hundred feet high) are but two of the man-made sights in Scotland worth seeing; others are the thirty-two steel lattice masts and ten square miles of Cupar Radio, and the many great reservoirs of which the Spean and Treig dams form the most extensive. The mountain passes of Scotland too are legion, one of the most dramatic being Killiecrankie, where "Bonnie Dundee" was killed in the hour of victory. Glencoe, where the Campbells brought deathless dishonor to their name by the murder of their hosts, the Macdonalds, is a National Trust scenic sanctuary.

> "Bring here" he said "the mazers four
> My noble fathers loved of yore.
> Thrice let them circle round the board,
> The pledge, fair Scotland's rights restored!
> And he whose lip shall touch the wine,
> Without a vow as true as mine,
> To hold both lands and life at nought,
> Until her freedom shall be brought,—
> Be brand of a disloyal Scot,
> And lasting infamy his lot!
> (Speech of the Bruce in
> *Lord of the Isle* by Sir Walter Scott)

IRELAND

"Come and daunce with me in Ireland," sang an Irish minstrel in the fourteenth century. In the twentieth, many still do, and to the same old airs. The Irish dress like Americans or English, speak the same language, eat the same food, and enjoy the same drinks. "Yet every English visitor in Ireland," says Stephen Gwyn, "cries out at the unfamiliarity of everything." And he goes on to explain, "We are not endowed with great mountains, but those we have are so placed as to make the most of themselves. Mountains and plains —we have these, as we have also the hummocky land of our northern counties. But, above all the beauty of Ireland is the beauty of waters. The sea to begin with. . . . Then the fresh water. Ireland is above all the land of lakes [there are around 800]. And wherever a man is brought up in Ireland he has some river to fall in love with." A sportsman's country is Ireland—the trout and salmon fishing are superb, so are the pheasant, quail, and duck shooting: fine horses and hunting and racing are a tradition; hurling and Gaelic football are unique.

The Emerald Isle (the Republic covers 27,137 square miles of the island's total of 32,500) is like a reversible coat; wherever you go, there is the Ireland of the Irish and the Ireland of the conquerors, be they Danish or English, and both provide wonderful sights. One of the most extraordinary is the natural GIANT'S CAUSEWAY near Dunseverick Castle in Antrim. This bed of columnar basalt, formed by the "cooling of lava which burst through the earth's crust in the Cainozoic Period," has three main sections or causeways; and various formations have folksy names like the Wishing Chair, the Organ, or the Lady's Fan. Also in Ulster is Belfast, a big manufacturing city, boasting of "the biggest shipyard, the biggest spinning factory, the biggest tobacco factory and the biggest rope-works in Europe." It also has an excellent theater—the Ulster Players. It is handy for Bangor, with its wonderful sailing, and Armagh, which Daire the king gave Saint Patrick, and Portrush, called the metropolis of golf for the north of Ireland.

Down, also in the north, is one of Ireland's most fertile counties. The mountains of Mourne, massed in the broad peninsula between Dundrum Bay and Carlingford Lough, provide excellent tours around Newcastle and Kilkeel. GREENCASTLE, once the capital of the kingdom of Mourne, is as peaceful now as it was turbulent during the days when the Norman castle actively guarded the entrance to Carlingford Lough. Another Greencastle is in Donegal, one of the most famous holiday regions in Ireland. At Lough Derg is Saint Patrick's Purgatory, famous pilgrimage site, rivaled only by Croagh Patrick, the holy mountain in County Mayo.

Everywhere, from Londonderry to Tipperary, from Kildare to Limerick, are the lovely whitewashed and thatch-roofed FARMSTEADS and fertile fields joined together like patchwork quilts. In the tourist country of the south, first, there is BLARNEY CASTLE, with the Kissing Stone, five miles from the busy city of Cork:

The groves of Blarney they look so charming
Down by the purling of sweet silent brooks
(R. A. Milliken)

Nearby is Kinsale, where William Penn once lived. To the west, County Kerry, with its pagan and Christian monuments and beautiful scenery, is full of enchantment. Here is the grandeur of Killarney, and the Iveragh Peninsula with the coves of Dingle Bay. The hills around Glenbeigh provide some of the finest walks in the country, and at ROSSBEIGH STRAND the swimming is excellent.

All along the western coast the sea spray leaps three hundred feet above the cliffs; and the small ARAN ISLANDS, where the rugged islanders cling to their Gaelic traditions and make their soil with sand and seaweed, stoically face the brunt of the Atlantic. Here, and on Achill, J. M. Synge, the bittersweet playwright, got much of the conversation he uses.

Dublin, largely eighteenth century (when it became one of the great capitals of Europe), makes room for modern progress amid the architectural memories of a stirring and poetic history.

The Danes founded the church on whose site Christ Church Cathedral stands. In 1166 Dermot MacMurrough, king of Leinster, who was banished by the Irish chieftans, called the Norman-Welsh to his aid, and from 1171, when Henry II entered Dublin, to the "Peace by Treaty" of 1921, the king of England was king of Ireland, and Dublin was its capital. The Normans built Saint Patrick's Cathedral, bigger than Christ Church; both were restored in the last century through the munificence of publicminded distillers.

Trinity College has a copy, by right, of every book printed in English; bronze statues of Grattan, Burke, and Goldsmith, who were alumni, are outside. Grattan faces Trinity, standing outside the building that in his day was Ireland's House of Parliament, and is now the Bank of Ireland.

Dublin belongs above all to two men—to Dean Swift and James Joyce. To them even more than to A.E., who lived on Merion Square, or "Willie" Yeats, who filled the Senate and the Kildare Street Club with good talk. Or even than to Lady Gregory, who worked so hard to found the Abbey Theatre, as did Synge, who asked for his hospital bed to be moved as he lay dying so that he could once more see from the windows the hills of Kildare. Seventeen hundred and sixty acres of beautiful grassland comprise Phoenix Park, for the most part flat, yet at points sinking into adorable dingle, and nowhere a dead level, with playing fields of every kind. Beyond the ground rises the long, rolling mass of the Dublin Hills checkered with cloud shadows. The Lane Collection of pictures in the city's National Gallery is superb, and both theaters —the Abbey and the Gate—are worth visiting, and more than once. Other sights are the General Post Office, completed in 1818, which served as headquarters of the Irish Republican Army during the 1916 insurrection, and Dublin Castle, dating back to the thirteenth century.

Of Tara, once the religious, political, and cultural center of Ireland, there is little left but three fields, full of green mounds, a church of no special distinction, and a modern statue of Saint Patrick. Near Tara, however, is Kells, where a small building still stands, the remains of the monastery founded by Saint Columba, and where the Book of Kells, one of Ireland's greatest treasures, was written in the middle of the sixth century.

In Wicklow, a short distance south of Dublin, is Enniskerry, perhaps the prettiest village in the whole of Ireland. And nearby is the magnificent 34,000-acre estate of Viscount Powerscourt, which served as the background for the filming of Shakespeare's *Henry V*. Powerscourt House is built on the site of the former castle of the O'Tooles, Irish lords of Glencullen. Within the estate, POWERSCOURT WATERFALL tumbles obliquely over a four hundred foot cliff.

GLENDALOUGH, the Glen of the Two Lakes, with 2000-foot mountains rising from their sides, is the "desert" to which Saint Kevin came. It has, in all, seven churches, one of which is the lovely Saint Kevin's kitchen, or church. In a cave by the upper lake is the saint's bed where, legend has it, a young woman came to tempt him, but he pushed her out into the water. The REEFERT CHURCH there is the burial place of the O'Tooles.

It's still "a long way to Tipperary" and to CASHEL of the kings of Munster. On Cashel's great rock is the roofless cathedral, the tenth-century ROUND TOWER, King Cormac's Chapel, and Saint Patrick's Cross, honoring the saint who visited Cashel in 450. Nothing is left of the first cathedral founded in 1169. Gerald, earl of Kildare in 1495, "excused himself to Henry VII for burning the cathedral—because he thought the archbishop was inside!"

From the DUBLIN HORSE SHOW and the Curragh races to fishing in "the little bog-holes and tarns," each of which is stocked with trout, there is activity in Ireland as well as beauty for every visitor. And if any man desires to pursue European civilization as a whole from its beginnings, then Ireland is a good quarry. For here is design in stone from Chi-Rho symbols to Romanesque and Gothic, here were trained the Greek scholars who in the Carolingian renaissance—around 800—brought Greek back from Ireland to Europe, to such places as Saint Gallen and Lerins.

I found in Munster unfettered of any
Kings and queens and poets a many;
I found in Connacht the just redundance
Of riches, milk in lavish abundance;
I found in Ulster, from hill to glen,
Hardy warriors, resolute men;
I found in Leinster the smooth and sleek,
From Dublin to Slewmargy's peak;

I found in Meath's fair principality
Virtue, vigor and hospitality;
I found strict morals in age and youth.
I found historians recording truth.

(King Alfred's song upon leaving Ireland.)

FRANCE

"Every man has two countries, his own and France." This saying is so old no one knows who said it and so true no one, of any nationality, has ever denied it. Keyserling wrote that France embodies the one universally intelligible and universally enjoyable harmony between man and his surroundings that is to be found in Europe. The natural features of France are those of a garden. And every Frenchman is, first and foremost, a gardener, a cultivator. For what is a garden but cultivated nature? And what is morality but cultivated nature? To be a cultivator means to affirm life, and this the Frenchman does, with all his five senses. To be a moralist is to be a cultivator, and this also a Frenchman essentially is.

France with its 212,659 square miles, lived in by some 42,000,000 people is bigger than any other European country except Russia (but Texas is nearly as big as France and western Germany put together). It is favorably situated, being almost at the center of the world's land areas, yet bounded on three sides by the sea. Ethnically, land routes have linked France through Belgium with northern, central, and eastern Europe, through the Belfort Gap with the upper Rhine, and via the Danube with the Near East. The Pyrenees divide the country from Spain on the southwest, the Alps from Switzerland and Italy on the southeast, while the Ardennes and Vosges extend the line of the Alps northward. Only in the northeast is France pitifully vulnerable, as 1814, 1870, 1914, and 1940 all showed.

Normandy and Brittany have cool summers and mild winters, with plenty of rain, clouds, and fogs. Here is wonderful dairy country as well as orchard and market-gardening land, but not warm enough for grain or vines. The people of Normandy look rather English, and so does the landscape and the architecture of the churches, as such examples as Coutances, Avranches, and Caen clearly show. But considering, as a Virginian traveling in 1776 wrote, "how short is the time which transported us to a new world of manners, continual commercial intercourse might soften the angle of difference between the inhabitants of Calais and Dover: the very contrary is the fact. . . . When I crossed the Atlantic at the distance of two thousand miles, I found myself at home in England, the same style of living, the same language, the same manners. Here the difference was extreme, the tall meagre, perpendicular French soldier, on the ramparts of Calais, seemed of a species quite distinct from the fat-eyed, rubicund, citizen of Dover."

And it is in northern France that the great historical happenings occurred. From Germany the early settlers poured into northern France, the Norsemen came to Normandy, the great wars were first with England, then with Germany. England and France face each other as if on two sides of a valley, with the Channel as its ditch. "England," it is said, "offers her German front to France, she hides her Celts, of Wales, Scotland and Ireland. France, on the other hand, offers her Celtic front to England."

For Brittany is Celtic still, with her simplicity, her fern-named cities (like Fougères, which means "bracken"), her language so kin to Gaelic that Breton onion sellers peddling in Scotland chat with the natives there,

her melancholy seaports of Brest, Saint-Malo, Nantes. Brittany is the country of resistance; here the royalists fought to the last ditch after 1789; here in World War II the Germans were most afraid. Saint-Malo, Vannes, and, above all, MONT-SAINT-MICHEL—with its eighth-century abbey, a miracle of compression, built layer upon layer, tier upon tier, on a rocky island, seabound at the neap tides—are fortresses.

The strange menhirs in Brittany are megalithic stone monuments whose purpose is still unknown. The largest collection of menhirs is at Carnac; there are in all 2935, some over twelve feet high, and extending over a mile. Hardly less impressive are the Calvaries—that of PLOUGASTEL-DAOULAS, in the extreme west of the Armorican peninsula, was built in 1602-1604 to celebrate the cessation of the plague of 1598. Guimiliau, whose Calvary is older, has two hundred statuettes illustrating the life of Christ.

Normandy is more jocund, though it suffered more than Brittany in World War II. Le Havre, Cherbourg, Lisieux, Morlaix, and Falaise were all variously hurt, but each has a full quota of memorable remains. Falaise where William the Conqueror was born, and DIVES, where his INN flourishes, are charming. And the great Norman cathedrals—Beauvais, a sort of ark on Ararat, as John Ruskin called it, with its "indomitable spring of arch of unreachable height, and its huge expanses of dark glass, spotted with ruby and jacynth"; Amiens, whose Cathedral the same Ruskin called the Bible of Amiens, for so much of scripture is carved upon it (he insisted it was the finest Gothic in the world); Rouen, where the Maid burned; Le Mans and Soissons, glories to be seen; and Solesmes, where some of the best church music in the world can be heard.

PARIS, T. G. Appleton said, is where good Americans go when they die. Most don't wait. As a result, in the center of Paris, English is heard spoken to a surprising extent; as Pan American's *New Horizons* notes: "Almost every Frenchman not only can understand English but can now even understand an American trying to speak French." Paris has, of course, something for everyone; indeed, much for most people. The two islands, inhabited for over two thousand years, are its seed and kernel; and most people agree that the Ile de la Cité, with NOTRE DAME brooding over it like some gigantic, benign prehistoric creature, and the Ile Saint Louis, are two of the nicest places in the world. The Sainte Chapelle, built by Saint Louis in 1247-1250, is a lovely empty shell, incongruously beached when the waters of faith receded.

Just walking the streets is the best way to see Paris, whether one follows the Roman road, now the Rue Saint Jacques, or that other, now the Rue Saint Martin, through the Halles, or the Champs Elysées from the Arc de Triomphe through the Rond Point to the PLACE DE LA CONCORDE. Here the guillotine did its work: Louis XVI was killed, and his Austrian queen—so also were countless others. When the butchery was over the widened square was renamed. Every vocation has its location: *couture* in and around the Rue de la Paix, artists along the Left Bank and in the steep high streets of Montmartre (topped, as though with most expensive sugar icing, by the SACRÉ COEUR), theater around the Comédie Française, the secondhand books in the BOOKSTALLS along the SEINE, and art dealers along the Rue des Saints-Pères and Rue du Bac.

The university is where it has been since the twelfth century when it began on Saint Geneviève's Mount. Between 1150 and 1350 every scholar worth his salt in the civilized world came here. "O Paris. Queen among cities, Moon among stars! Happy city, where the students are so numerous their multitude almost surpasses that of the other inhabitants!" was their cry to her, and Richard de Bury, Bishop of Durham, wrote before 1350 of the mighty stream of pleasure which made glad his heart whenever he visited what is now the Latin Quarter. The LOUVRE contains the most famous of all Leonardo da Vinci's paintings, the "Mona Lisa," of which Walter Pater wrote: "Here is the head upon which all the ends of the world are come, and the eyelids are a little weary. It is a beauty wrought out from within upon the flesh, the deposit, little cell by cell, of strange thoughts and fantastic reveries and exquisite

passions. Set it for a moment beside one of those white Greek goddesses . . . and how would they be troubled by this beauty into which the soul with all its maladies has passed?" The Louvre also contains one of the greatest of the white Greek goddesses: The "NIKE," or "Winged Victory," of Samothrace. Of her, less contemptuously than Walter Pater, the poet Rainer Maria Rilke wrote: "The wonderful movement and wide sea-wind in her garment is a miracle to me and like a whole world. . . . That is Greece. That is shore, sea and light, courage and victory." She stands on the stairs and at night is all lit up.

The Louvre, however, for all its treasures is but one of the many glorious museums and art galleries of Paris. Here are the Orangerie, the Petit Palais, and so many more. The Bibliothèque Nationale is wonderful, too. The gardens of Paris are an integral part of the city, not oases in it, or from it. The sudden burst of the Tuileries by the Louvre and from the RUE DE RIVOLI is one of the great sights, so are the Luxembourg Gardens, those of the Palais Royal, and, above all, the Bois de Boulogne, with its lakes and rides and paths. Here French children, civilized so young, play imaginatively and decorously beside their nurses, who sometimes still wear the funny *bécassine* bonnets.

No city in the world puts on better international expositions than Paris. It has had several. Although few open on the date advertised, sooner or later the fountains (a major attraction of every display) champagne forth, and the city bubbles over with excitement. The 1889 show left behind the EIFFEL TOWER which, although detested by aesthetes of the day, has worn surprisingly well and is still the gay symbol of modern Paris. The Palais de Chaillot at the top of Rue Kléber is a lively relic of the 1937 show, which was attended amidst great preliminary confusion by the Lord Mayor of London in his fairy-tale coach.

Outside Paris, as outside London, are some of the city's greatest treasures. VERSAILLES, twelve miles away, has unforgettable FOUNTAINS, and the gardens without and mirrors within the PALACE reflect the grandeur of its creator, Louis XIV. FONTAINEBLEAU, with its 42,200-acre forest and PALACE that Francis I built and Napoleon loved (and abdicated in); Chantilly, once the Prince of Condé's palace, thought by many to be finer than Versailles (certainly the stables are); Marly-le-Roi, where Louis XIV had his summer house; Ermenonville, where Jean Jacques Rousseau is buried on a small isle of poplars, by a lake whose "silence reposes on its bosom"; Neuilly, which is still forest; Saint-Germain-en-Laye, with a terrace three kilometers long; Senlis, with its twelfth-century Cathedral and Roman castle, its arena and two abbeys; Saint-Denis, where the kings and queens of France were buried, with a spectacular treasury, are all within easy reach of the city.

Compiègne, in its forest, was the scene of the signing of two surrenders: German in 1918, French in 1940. Rheims and Arras both have good cathedrals (Rheims, some experts claim, is even more nearly perfect than Chartres); and Nancy, with its eighteenth-century air, is a charming and unusual town. When General Mangin rode into Metz in 1918 he distributed to the troops copies of Paul Verlaine's patriotic poem on the enslavement of his native city; with Toul and Verdun, it has been one of three frontier posts since time began. It was George Duhamel, the writer, who declared in 1940 that in withdrawing behind the Maginot line France had lost the Descartes line—the intellectual ascendancy over the world.

The Loire country is full of *la douceur angevine,* the sweetness of Anjou, that lightest and loveliest of countries as of wines. Cézanne said the light was the hero of every country; it is certainly the hero of every French landscape from those Fouquet illuminated with his missal colors to Corot's avenues of poplar trees and Van Gogh's *passacaglias* of Provençal blossom. In the Loire valley the light is liquid silver, and the cities, Angers, Saumur, Tours, Blois, are sunny and sleepy; as Michelet put it, "here France loosens her belt, the Loire," here the country is lazy, uncorseted. Indeed the Loire is so sleepy it often just forgets which way it is

flowing, or to flow at all, lost in backwaters, among charming islands. The great castles are leisurely places: Francis I took twelve years building CHAMBORD, the greatest. Here women dominate history, Diane de Poitiers, Agnès Sorel, Catherine de Médicis, and earlier England's Queen Eleanor of Aquitaine who is buried in the great Romanesque church at Fontevrault.

Angers, which Henry James called "a sell . . . stupidly and vulgarly modernized" has, he admitted, a very old and large chateau; so big and so old that this simple impression is enough, and it takes its place in your recollections as a perfect specimen of a "superannuated stronghold." Tours won his louder praise: the beautiful Cathedral possessing "a charming mouse-colored complexion and a pair of fantastic towers. There are many grander cathedrals, but there are probably few more pleasing, and this effect of delicacy and grace is at its best towards the close of a quiet afternoon, when the densely decorated towers lift their curious lanterns into the slanting light."

BLOIS, on the north bank of the Loire, is dominated by the CATHEDRAL and the graceful chateau, with its gay red brick, crowded here and there with purple. The wing of the chateau built by Francis I is altogether delightful, with the famous winding staircase rising from the middle of it, "a kind of chiseled cylinder, with wide interstices, so that the stairs are open to the air." Arthur Young, writing in 1788, also comments on Blois's good stone bridge of eleven arches, but dismisses its history: "the character of the period, and of the men that figured in it, were alike disgusting. . . . The parties could hardly be better employed than in cutting each other's throats." Blois's most famous murder took place in the chateau when the all-powerful Henry, Duc de Guise, through the plotting of Henry III, was put away just before Christmas, 1588. Chambord more than answered Young's expectations, while rococo Cheverny, built in 1634, he called a light, sweet mansion, with a quite perfect formal garden. Amboise, halfway between Blois and Tours, has an admirable bridge, and "the town is so small, the pedestal so big, and the castle so high and striking that the clustered houses at the base of the rock are like the crumbs that have fallen from a well-laden table."

Jean Jacques Rousseau spent the fall of 1747 in the royal Château of Chenonceaux, which had been given by Henry II to Diane de Poitiers. "We amused ourselves greatly at this fine place," he wrote in his *Confessions,* "the living was of the best, and I became as fat as a monk." Built in 1515, Chenonceaux is two stories high, with a high-pitched roof and an enchanting bridge which forms two corridors across the Cher. Azay-le-Rideau, Chaumont, Chinon, and the grim Loches, with revolting memorials of man's inhumanity to man, are all fuller of history than a comb of honey.

CHARTRES, for the twentieth century, has become more than a cathedral; it is a symbol of all that is Gothic, indeed of all the ages of faith. The windows, taken out in wartime, are for us like the gates of Janus in Rome. When the gates were shut, when the windows are up, we cry peace, like Zimri. Our writers have done Chartres proud; Henry Adams' classic book and James Russell Lowell's sonnet wear well.

I stood before the triple northern post,
Where dedicated shapes of saints and
      kings,
Stern faces bleared with immemorial
      watch,
Look down benignly grave. . . .

Not far from Chartres is ETAMPES, also in the fruitful district of Beauce; and some forty miles south of it, in Loiret, ORLÉANS feasts Saint Joan, in May. The CATHEDRAL towers of Sainte Croix, built after Calvinist damages to the structure in 1567, suffered a hit in the last World War, but the Cathedral with its wonderful wood carvings is still lovely. And in the rich Burgundy country, south to southeast of Paris, there is so much to be drunk that perhaps some of the things to be seen might be neglected. Pontigny and Vézelay should *not* be.

The south begins at AVIGNON, with the PALACE OF THE POPES, and their bridge; Villeneuve across the Rhone, and Tarascon and Beaucaire. Tarascon is as famous for

Tartarin and his boasting as for Saint Martha's dragon, the Tarasque, which appears, in effigy, once a year. Beaucaire is the castle where Aucassin lived—Nicolette's boy friend in one of the earliest of French love stories. Love stories are all important here for, as E. M. Forster said, all feelings grow to passions in the south. Vaucluse, the shut valley where Petrarch lived and immortalized his love for Laura, has been described by Leigh Hunt: "Here he thought to forget his passion for Laura, and here he found it stronger than ever. We do not well see how it could have been otherwise, for Laura lived no great way off, at Chabrières, and he appears to have seen her often in the very place." Henry James is more romantic: "The protrusion of the mountain shuts it in, and you penetrate to the bottom of the recess which they form. You leave the little booths and stalls behind, but the bescribbled crag, bristling with human vanity, keeps you company even when you stand face to face with the fountain. This happens when you find yourself at the foot of the enormous straight cliff out of which the river gushes. It rears itself to an extraordinary height—a huge forehead of bare stone. The little valley, seeing it there, stops suddenly and receives in its arms the magical spring. . . . From under the mountain it silently rises, without visible movement, filling a small natural basin with the stillest blue water." This sight inspired Sir Winston Churchill to paint, as well as many great and lesser artists.

Roman France has splendid cities, of which the best are Besançon, Narbonne, Arles, Nîmes, and Orange. Nîmes is the grandest. It has Roman baths, with an adjacent temple of Diana; the strange Tour Magne, described as a dateless tube; the ARENA, a small colosseum in better preservation than the one at Rome; and, above all, the Maison Carrée, a temple that rivals Paestum or Segesta for perfection (Stendhal remarked it was the shape of a playing card). The Pont du Gard, ten miles away, is a perfectly preserved Roman aqueduct; nothing has crumbled or collapsed. The number of arches in each tier is different. Of honey-colored blocks of stone, they pile up, without cement or mortar, just as neatly as when first the aqueduct was built.

ARLES has the most beautiful women, it is said, in France; it also has the most melancholy avenue in the world, the Alyscamps. Many know Arles for its arena and Roman theater; still others through the eyes of Van Gogh, who painted so much of it. The native costumes are charming, and so are the whitewashed and thatch-roofed farmsteads in the neighboring countryside, approached along characteristic roads lined with poplars. Aix-en-Provence probably has the most fountains of any city of comparable size, every street beginning or ending in one. The splashing is a cool sound alike under the heavy plane trees of the Cours Mirabeau or in the narrow side streets. Aix, of course, spells Cézanne, whose little house is kept as he left it. On the sea, Aiguesmortes, the walled city from which Saint Louis sailed to the Crusade, and Saintes Maries, where Martha, Mary, and their maid Sara, the patroness of gypsies, are supposed to have landed, are both slightly sinister, set in uncultivated flats, the home of flamingoes, and wild white horses and bulls.

A hidden gem of Aveyron is the secluded village of CONQUES on a tributary of the Lot, where beautiful sculptures and church treasures, some a thousand years old, may be found in the eleventh-century Romanesque church of Sainte-Foy, once a part of one of the richest abbeys of the Middle Ages.

CARCASSONNE, medieval walled city wonderfully restored by Viollet-le-Duc, gives much the same impression as Colonial Williamsburg from the point of view of flawless preservation. It is at the beginning of the Pyrenees, the home of the BASQUE people with their unspoiled villages, folk dancing, and song.

The Riviera begins east of Marseilles; and the three great roads, the Petite Corniche, Moyenne Corniche, and the Grande Corniche, go through country you thought was true only on postcards. The nightingales shout so in May and June you can hear them above your car engine's purring. Here is the playground of the world: here are CANNES, Nice, VILLEFRANCHE, MONTE CARLO, Mentone, Antibes. And behind it, as behind the English South Coast sea resorts, is wonderful unspoiled country where famous painters such as Picasso, Matisse and others have lived or still do. Fragonard had a home at Grasse, Renoir at Cagnes. Further back still are the real Alps and Savoy, a kingdom until 1870 and still very much to itself.

In Savoy are such dramatically beautiful places as CHAMONIX, with Mont Blanc, the highest peak in Europe, towering above it, and the GRANDE CHARTREUSE, where, in complete silence and utter solitude from the time the Carthusian order was founded there in 1084 monks lived the severest of all rules among superb mountain peaks. In Savoy, too, are Aix-les-Bains on Lake Bourget, the lake of Lamartine's poem; Lake Annecy; and, north, the Lake of Geneva. To the west, in Haute-Loire, is Le Puy, particularly noted for its shrine of Notre-Dame, one of the most famous places of pilgrimage, visited by Charlemagne among others; and for the ROCHER D'AIGUILLE on the outskirts, a volcanic wonder, with the tenth century church of Saint Michel d'Aiguille on top.

To the north, and on the extreme eastern border of France, is STRASBOURG, where the Marseillaise was first sung. The city has shuttled to and fro; it was German, now is French. The chief attraction is the majestic CATHEDRAL which still stands at the end of Rue Mercière. It was eulogized by Goethe, who studied law at the university in 1770-1771.

France is all these places and so many more, gathered up into one of the most complete identities Europe has ever known. It still retains more than a smattering of fraternity and quite a good showing, all things considered, of liberty and equality.

Bill Brandt

tonehenge, Salisbury Plain, Wiltshire, the most important relic of prehistoric times in England.

Allan Cash

J. Allan Cash

Above: Bath, Somerset. Robert Adam's Pulteney Bridge. Samuel Pepys, Jane Austen, and many others have written about this beautiful city, famous for its Roman baths and Georgian architecture.

Right: The Cat and the Fiddle inn at Hinton Admiral, in the New Forest, Hampshire, near Christchurch.

Opposite, top: Village street and inn at Winsford, Somerset.

Opposite: Clovelly cottages cling to the cliffs above Barnstaple Bay, Devonshire, as they did in Dickens' time.

Knole, Kent, with its 365 rooms, is one of the best known of the great English houses.

White Cliffs. The Seven Sisters, Sussex, at end of the South Downs, are much like those at Dover.

Hurstmonceaux, the fifteenth-century castle near Eastbourne, Sussex, built in the reign of Henry VI.

Canterbury, Kent, chief see of the Church of England. The cathedral was founded in 597.

W. F. Manse

Fritz Henle

B.I.S.

London. *Opposite page:* Houses of Parliament, with Big Ben at right. *Bottom, left:* Bobby on duty in Piccadilly Circus. *Bottom, right:* Her Majesty, Queen Elizabeth II, with the Duke of Edinburgh leaving Buckingham Palace for the state opening of Parliament.

Right: Unique shop in the heart of the capital.

Below: The Tower of London, founded by Julius Caesar, was rebuilt and added to in later centuries. Anne Boleyn, Sir Thomas More, and scores of other noted prisoners were executed here. To the right, Tower Bridge, a Victorian landmark.

Bernd Lohse

London. Saint Paul's Cathedral Christopher Wren's masterpiece.

Below: Windsor Castle. Berkshire The sovereign's palace, near London rebuilt by Edward III, towers over the town of Shakespeare's *Merry Wives.*

Oxford. Magdalen Tower, designed by Cardinal Wolsey while he was bursar of the college.

Cambridge. The "Bridge of Sighs" at Saint John's College, over the "backs."

41

Anne Hathaway's Cottage, and garden, in Shakespeare's Stratford on Avon, Warwickshire.

Sulgrave Manor, Helmdon, Northamptonshire, the home of George Washington's ancesto

Henri Cartier-Bresson

Window display in the ancient town of Ludlow, Shropshire.

posite, top: Conway Castle, Caer-
rvonshire, Wales, built by Edward
n 1284 in his offensive to subdue
orth Wales. The suspension bridge
s added in 1826.

posite, bottom: Plas Newydd, the
house of the "blue stocking" ladies
Llangollen, Denbighshire, Wales.

ght: Ely Cathedral. The Isle of Ely,
the center of the Fen district, was
e of the last strongholds to surren-
to William the Conqueror.

low: Traditional Morris Dancers at
nchingfield, one of the prettiest
sex villages .

Combine

J. Allan Cash

George E. Pickow

Richmond, Yorkshire. The Grammar School, founded by Elizabeth I. To t[...]
south lies the moors which the Brontës made so famous. *Below:* Huntsm[...]
going to the meet, a familiar sight in all the shires.

Henri Cartier-Bress[...]

COTLAND

W. Suschitzky

inburgh Castle seen from Princes Street in the morning mist.

Combine

European

Above: In the Trossachs, Loch Katri
and Ellen's Isle, Perthshire, the setti
of Sir Walter Scott's *Lady of the Lak*

Left: Highland sword dance at Edi
burgh Castle.

Opposite, top: Holyrood Palace, t
Queen's Edinburgh residence, whe
Rizzio, Mary Queen of Scots' lov
was murdered. In the eighteenth ce
tury, Bonnie Prince Charlie danc
in its halls while the British foug
him at Edinburgh Castle.

Opposite: The great Glen More fro
Invergarry over Loch Oich to Lo
Ness, Inverness-shire.

48

J. Allan Cash

Above: Glenfinnan, Inverness-shire with statue of Bonnie Prince Charlie, Stuart pretender to the British throne.

Left: Sheep in the Scottish Highlands.

Opposite, top: Cathedral at Iona, Argyllshire, in the Hebrides; the island where Macbeth, Duncan, and other kings lie buried, was the great center of Gaelic Christianity.

Fritz Henle

B.R.

RELAND

...ant's Causeway, Antrim, the extra-
...dinary promontory of natural basalt
...ck pillars at Benbane Head on the
...rth coast of Ireland.

J. Allan Cash

Everywhere in the Emerald Isle are neatly cultivated fields and simple whitewashed farmsteads.

Greencastle, Down, old capital of the Kingdom of Mourne. The Norman Castle was built to guard the entrance of Carlingford Lough.

Fógra Fáilte

Loading turf on the rugged Aran Islands off the west coast of Ireland.

Blarney Castle, Cork, built in 1446 by Cormac McCarthy, contains the stone that "confers eloquence on all who kiss it."

Fógra Fáilte

Rossbeigh Strand, Kerry, curves
under the shadows of Curra Hill,
near Glenbeigh, on Dingle Bay.

The Dublin Horse Show, a leading event in the capital. General
view of the jumping enclosure.

I.T.A.

Fógra Fá

W. *Suschitzky*

Waterfall at Powerscourt, Wicklow, on the 34,000 acre estate where Shakespeare's *Henry V* was filmed.

Fógra Fáilte

Glendalough, Wicklow, near Dubli[n] associated with Saint Kevin, a[nd] noted for its ecclesiastic ruins. T[he] graveyard at Reefert Church, buri[al] place of the O'Tooles.

Cashel, Tipperary. The Round To[wer] from the Cathedral. O'Brien, Kin[g of] Limerick, paid homage to Henry [II at] Cashel, and Edward Bruce held [an] Irish parliament here.

I.T.A.

Martin Hürlimann

Calvary of Plougastel-Daoulas, Finistère, Brittany, erected 1602–1604 to
commemorate the end of the 1598 plague.

Below: The old Inn of William the Conqueror at Dives, Normandy.

pposite: Mont-Saint-Michel, island sanctuary and fortress off the Brittany and Nor-andy coast, is one of the most revered places in France.

W. Suschitzky

Paris from the top of Notre Dame Cathedral. The Sacré Coeur is on the hill at distant left.

Paris. Fishing on the Seine near the Cathedral.

Left: Outdoor bookstall, on the quay.

Opposite: Artist Picasso's Paris studio.

Brassai

P. Joly

Paris. *Left:* View of the Seine from Notre Dame. *Below:* Rue Bonaparte from Boulevard Saint-Germain.

Tod Webb (Ess

mbine

Paris. *Above:* Rue de Rivoli. At extreme left is the house of Baron de Rothschild. *Right:* The Greek Nike ("Victory of Samothrace") in the Louvre.

Marcel Louchet

Tom Maloney

Paris. *Above:* In the Louvre. *Left:*
The Eiffel Tower, symbol of Paris
since the exposition of 1889.

F.T.O.

64

Paris. Fireworks over Sacré
Coeur during Bastille Day cele-
brations, July 14. *Below:* Sidewalk café near Place de l'Opera.

Lucien Viguier

Fritz Henle

65

Fritz Henle

Paris. Night illuminations, Place de la Concorde. *Opposite, top:* Fountains at Versaille
Opposite: Palace of Fontainebleau, Seine-et-Marne, a favorite resort of French kings.

Versailles Palace. Originated by Louis XIV, the Sun King, it remained a royal residence unt
the overthrow of Louis XVI and Marie Antoinette. The fountains in the garden are shown o
the previous page.

Fritz Henle

Sylvain Knecht

ight view of Château Chambord, Loir-et-Cher, the greatest of the Loire châteaux, started by
rancis I (1526), and completed by Henry II. Molière's *Le Bourgeois gentilhomme* premièred
re.

Opposite: Street viewed from the cathedral in Chartres, Eure-et-Loir.

Opposite, bottom: Blois, chief town of the department Loir-et-Cher, famous for its Cathedral and historic château where the powerful Duc de Guise was murdered in 1588.

Right: Orléans, Loiret. The Cathedral in the town besieged by the English in 1428–1429 and relieved by Joan of Arc during the Hundred Years' War.

Below: A charming restaurant on the Chartres road, near Etampes, Seine-et-Oise.

Ewing Galloway

71

W. Suschitzky

72

Opposite: Avignon, Vaucluse. Palace of the Popes, used during the "Babylonian Captivity" of the Church (1309–1367). Across the Rhone is the famous "pont."

Right: A young couple on their way to the fete at Arles, Bouches-du-Rhône.

Below: Nîmes. The Arena, built in the time of Augustus, is one of the many splendid Roman remains in this prosperous chief town of Gard.

Suschitzky

Yan

73

Martin Hürlimann

Conques, Aveyron, a beautiful, secluded village on a tributary of the river Lo

T.O.

Karquel

arcassone, Aude, at foot of
e Pyrenees, with its walls,
ttlements, castle, and tow-
s, is France's most per-
ctly restored medieval for-
ess.

ancers in the southern
asque country, in the re-
ion of the Pyrenees.

Ewing Krainin

Monte Carlo, the fabulous international resort on the Riviera

Deane Dickason

Villefranche (*above*) and Cannes (*below*), also on the beautiful Côte d'Azur.

Ivan Dmitri

(American Export Lines)

Chamonix, Haute-Savoie, in the French Alps. Nearby is Mont Blanc, Europe's highest peak.

tside Le Puy, chief town of Haute-Loire department, is the Rocher d'Aiguille, with the Xth-
ntury church on top of the strange volcanic prominence.

Burton Holmes

posite: The Grande Chartreuse in the lower Alps of the Dauphine, near Grenoble, Isère.
t Bruno founded the Carthusian order here in 1084.

Martin Hürlimann

Strasbourg, Bas-Rhin. West front of the magnificent Gothic Cathed

BELGIUM

Culturally, the Low Countries are a Germano-Latin frontier. Belgium emphasizes the Latin, Holland the German aspect of this bonded civilization; they have actually, historically, much in common, but in every other way—socially, psychologically, even geographically, they are very different. Belgium has a population of some nine million, packed into a country roughly the size of Maryland—nowhere are its frontiers as much as 200 miles apart. Brussels, the capital, is big—over a million and a quarter population. By air, Brussels is little over an hour from Paris; by boat, a long week from the United States to Antwerp or very comfortably overnight from London to OSTEND via Dover (the ferry takes automobiles, too). The country has recovered from two world wars, economically and emotionally, better than most other countries, and there has been large-scale industrial development.

Belgium speaks two languages, Dutch (Flemish) in Flanders, the northern part, and French in Wallonia, or the south. These languages represent two entirely different racial strains, Latin and Germanic. A charming story is told of the ex-Crown Princess of Piedmont, the present King of Belgium's aunt. On her first morning at boarding school her companions waited with baited breath: would she crack her egg at the big end or the little? The Flemish girls hoped the one, the Walloons the other. The tactful schoolgirl princess ate her egg *à l'américaine,* shelling it into a cup.

Ten miles from the center of Brussels, WATERLOO is hardly today the dreary plain Victor Hugo called it. On the contrary, all around is rather pretty undulating country. The delightful monument, near the church, of the Marquis of Anglesey to his leg, amputated immediately after the battle that vanquished Napoleon, is under a weeping willow. Mechelen (Malines), with its clock-conscious cathedral, has a magnificent Van Dyck crucifixion, in the church of Saint John a ceremonial Rubens, and in Notre Dame the latter's "Miraculous Draught of Fishes."

Mechelen, like Brussels, is famous for fine lace, and here as everywhere in Belgium one eats too well. An old Latin tag has it that Brussels rejoices in noble men, Antwerp in money, Ghent in halters (from the number of its patriots who have been hanged), Louvain in wise men, and Mechelen in fools. The tale is told that one night the moonlight so burnished Mechelen's tower that the city fathers, fearing their steeple on fire, tried to put out the moon!

BRUSSELS, on the great commercial route between Bruges and Cologne, was important as early as the eighth century. The "dwelling on the march," rebuilt in 1731 after a fire, is divided between the upper town, where are the Parliament, ministries and private houses, and the downtown or business section. The Park is particularly lovely, with the Royal Palace and the modern Palais de Justice built 1866-1883. Almost square, it is said to have been inspired by Assyrian forms. The GRANDE PLACE where the Hôtel de Ville, Broodhuis, and some of the guild houses still stand, the heart of the city, is a perfect example of a medieval square. The Hôtel de Ville, begun in 1402, is unique, with its open spire, surmounted by a gilded Archangel Michael. Inside, the magnificence of the ceiling paintings and the tapestries, both designed by Victor Janssens, recalls the Palace of the Doges in Venice. The Manneken Fountain, cast in bronze in 1619, is a kind of city mascot and is dressed up on popular feasts and political occasions.

Saint Gudule, the Cathedral in Brussels, is a singularly fine specimen of pointed Gothic. It was begun about 1220, but not finished until the fifteenth century. The stained glass windows are famous, and contain figures of members of the houses of Burgundy and Hapsburg. Particularly beautiful is the glass in the Chapel of the Sacrament.

Brussels is a most agreeable place to visit. The native language, the outdoor cafes and other Gallic touches make it seem rather like a neat and miniature Paris. The city is well laid out and owes much in this respect to nineteenth-century remodeling. The modern boulevards follow the course of old ramparts; and pleasant avenues lead out to

Laeken, for instance, where the public can see the king's gardens, and to the thickly populated suburbs.

ANTWERP was a great port in the sixteenth century, but after the religious wars the Treaty of Westphalia in 1648 closed the Schelde to navigation, and it was not re-opened until after the Congress of Vienna. Since then it has again become one of the leading European ports. The city possesses the largest and one of the best Gothic cathedrals in Belgium, begun in 1352. It also possesses some extremely fine works by Rubens (the painter returned to Antwerp in 1608 after his eight years in Italy). "The Adoration of the Magi," among others, is in the Royal Museum; the "Elevation of the Cross" and the "Descent from the Cross" are in the Cathedral. The Cathedral tower, like many in Belgium and the Netherlands, is only one-third of its intended height, but even so is almost too high for its own good. Napoleon compared it with Mechelen lace.

Antwerp's Hôtel de Ville, with its arcades—Doric and Ionian—resting on massive pillars, is lovely Renaissance, and many of the guild houses are beautiful examples of sixteenth- and seventeenth-century architecture. In the Church of Saint Jacob is Rubens' tomb, with the allegorical picture he did of himself and his family.

One of the loveliest and wateriest of European cities is BRUGES, which means "bridges." Once it was the pride of the old Hanseatic League, the successful rival of Venice as a canal town, and the richest in Europe. The Cathedral and Notre Dame, both Gothic, are full of admirable Flemish pictures. The Memlings in the Hospital of Saint John (notably Saint Ursula's shrine); the splendid belfry; the fourteenth-century Hôtel de Ville; the Chapel of the Holy Blood, in rich flamboyant style, and the almshouses; the Church of Jerusalem, which a good burgomaster, who died in 1483, made in imitation of the Holy Sepulcher, are all perfect settings for any medieval memory. As Robert Southey put it:

When I may read of tilts in days of old,
And tourneys graced by chieftains of renown,

Fair dames, grave citizens, and warriors bold,
If fancy would portray some stately town,
Which for such pomp fit theatre should be,
Fair Bruges, I shall then remember thee.

And D. G. Rossetti added:

I climbed at Bruges all the flight
The belfry has of ancient stone.
For leagues I saw the east wind blown;
The earth was grey. The sky was white.
I stood so near upon the height
That my flesh felt the carillon.

GHENT stretches over six miles and is the capital of Flanders. A turbulent city that has fought and suffered all the way through history, its Cathedral contains one of the greatest altarpiece decorations in existence, the van Eyck brothers' "Adoration of the Lamb," painted between 1420 and 1432 for Jodocus Vijdts and his wife, Isabella Burluut, of Ghent. The belfry, 375 feet high, with its gilded dragon vane, is worth climbing, not only to see the dark stairs, the square Gothic-windowed rooms, but also the beautiful view over Flanders. The oldest bell is inscribed: "My name is Roland; when I am rung hastily, there is a fire; when I burst forth in peals, there is a victory in Flanders." The Hôtel de Ville, the QUAI AUX HERBES, the CHATEAU, and the Béguinages (the big and the small) are all lovely.

Liége has big coal and iron industries; Louvain a great university. The prettiest country in Belgium is around Namur, where the Sambre River winds through green valleys, skirting wooded hills. At Namur itself the Sambre joins the Meuse, and from the citadel (fortified since Caesar's day) the view is like the background for any early Flemish picture, greeny-blue, with sudden cliffs. Along the Meuse are great country houses, such as Dave, Freyr, Namèche. Around Dinant there are fabulous caves, and almost everywhere in Belgium are battlefields—especially, of course, near Mons, Ypres, and many other of the smaller towns. Huy is picturesque, as is Chaudfontaine, a tiny watering place; and the towers of Franchimont,

Which like a eagle's nest in lair
Hang o'er the stream and hamlet fair

were sung by Sir Walter Scott. Spa, in the eighteenth century, was to Europe what Bath was to England. Under a precipitous mountain—the highest point of the Ardennes (over 2000 feet)—are chalybeate springs.

The Dutch-Belgian contrast, it has been said, "mirrors in miniature, within the framework of a family, the German-French contrast." Certainly great differences existed between the Flemish and the Dutch painters, even very early, and the correspondingly great differences between the Flemish and the French, the Dutch and the German, have been demonstrated in blood and water—the blood of the Resistance, the water of deliberately flooded lands—twice in this century, and countless times before. For all their quiet, serene landscapes, for all their concern for good, secure living, no two nations in the world have fought or suffered more. In contrast to their painters who loved to paint quiet interiors; the Belgians—from the Belgae who defied Caesar, and the burghers who defied the aristocracy throughout the Middle Ages, to the latter-day heroes who defied wave upon wave of German invasions —have loved to show that the bourgeoisie also has its heroes and its martyrs.

HOLLAND

Holland, even in Roman days, had its own culture. The Germanic Batavians and Frisians were courageous and freedom-loving peoples. The present-day Netherlanders still are, as the long drawn out years of internal resistance from May 1940 to May 1945 demonstrated.

The Dutch, a German has admitted, "are possessed of fixed emotions and cultural instinct which make them largely independent of external incident." Historic resistance to German, Frankish, and Spanish invasions has not alone accounted for their stoic nature. Of the thirteen thousand square miles that is Holland, nearly a quarter lies below the level of the North Sea—behind eternally threatened dikes. There is the old saying that "God made the Earth, except Holland, which

the Dutchmen made for themselves." And Dryden wrote:

"Then we upon our globe's last verge shall
  go
And see the ocean leaning on the sky"

Many people journey to Holland just to glimpse the bulb fields, particularly fine between Leyden and Haarlem. In springtime the scent and color are fantastic, great swathes of tulips, hyacinths, daffodils, narcissi are folded over the land like flags. TULIPS are as much a symbol of Holland as the wooden shoes (klompen), Dutch bonnets, windmills, or soap.

The Dutch "love of cleanliness sometimes amounts almost to a monomania. The scrubbing, washing and polishing which most houses undergo once every week, externally as well as internally, are occasionally somewhat subversive of comfort." Though Baedeker speaks so categorically, few would agree with him!

The architecture most readily associated with Holland stems from the sixteenth and seventeenth centuries. The houses, particularly those in Amsterdam, are mostly made of red brick and white cement. The beams frequently projecting from the gables are used for hoisting anything and everything to the upper floors. The Dutch are fond of light, so large windows are the rule, and they almost always have gay flower boxes. Dutch domesticity itself is gay, and clean, and shining. In many of the old cities the canals reflect back sky-light and sparkle. The modern buildings, of which there are many, are cleverly designed to blend with the old.

More fortunate than Rotterdam in the last war, DELFT is all the many seventeenth-century pictures of it have promised, full of clean canals and cleaner houses sunning themselves on their banks, and it is still the center for the manufacture of the lovely blue-and-white Delft pottery. Here William the Silent was murdered in 1584, and here, too, Hugo Grotius, the founder of the idea of neutrality, is buried.

The Hague, where the seat of government has existed since 1247, is fourteen miles away. Like Washington, it is a purely ministerial and diplomatic city. The queen has a palace at The Hague, though she lives mainly in the one at Soestdijk, and in the Knights' Hall opens Parliament each third Tuesday in September. In the Mauritshuis hang no less than sixteen Rembrandts, including the "Lesson in Anatomy," several self-portraits, a charming one of "Saskia," his wife, "Simeon in the Temple," and "Susannah and the Elders." Also on the walls is the lovely "Garden of Eden," half Rubens, half Brueghel, in front of which Charles Morgan had his lovers meet in *The Fountain.* "Then she went forward and sat down before Adam and Eve in Paradise. Her eyes sparkled as they moved from the golden flesh of Rubens' figures to the gracious smiling countryside that Breughel had painted. . . . Considering the work before her, she was aware of being received into it; as if walking between the apple tree and the coiled serpent into the enchanted glade she left her former self behind, asleep on the outskirts of the garden."

In The Hague is the PEACE PALACE, where the International Court of Justice is housed, the one branch of the League of Nations that still functions. The building was given by Andrew Carnegie, and the court is composed of fourteen elected members, representing different countries. One of the many disputes on the court calendar for 1953 was the one between France and England over possession of the tiny Minquiers Islands. The largest island measures a bare hundred by thirty-five yards at high tide. Britain claimed ownership (and the fruitful fishing rights) as a Norman inheritance rightfully theirs since 1066, and formally protested a Gallic invasion by the crews of seventeen fishing smacks who defiantly posted the sign: "Protected refuge of French seamen." Every yard of Europe has, at one time or another, belonged to some other nation, race, or clan; every foot has been fought for, given, or stolen.

LEYDEN, the Oxford of Holland and native town of Rembrandt, is on the Oude Rijn ("Old Rhine"). The *Lugdunum Batavorum* of Roman days, Leyden lost the last relic of that era in an eighteenth-century flood. The city is best known for its heroism during the Spanish siege of 1574, and for the university awarded the citizens a year later by William of Orange. In 1940, the faculty refused to compromise with the Nazis, and the university closed down. Today it thrives again with more than a thousand students. Hofjes, groups of small houses arranged around a courtyard and lived in rent free by old people, a characteristic Dutch institution, are numerous in Leyden. Typical also are the surrounding bulb fields and windmills, canals and waterways. In icy winters, hardy citizens take to the frozen canals on skates. The thirty-mile "Windmill Race" near Leyden is unique.

AMSTERDAM, the nation's economic capital, is as attractive a city as any you'll find, the CANALS everywhere making the old buildings, the bridges, the trees, the flower markets, the barges, and the piles of cheeses doubly colorful and important. Amsterdam's good humor, dignity, good sense, and courtesy make it memorable. The city, divided by its canals into ninety islands, has over three hundred bridges.

The old canals, the Prinsen Gracht, Keizer Gracht, and Heeren Gracht, in Amsterdam are all lined with trees and are wide and splendid. The houses along them are patrician, mostly dating from the seventeenth century. Seventy lesser *grachten,* all bordered with red-brick houses, connect with these main canals. (Erasmus, a native of Rotterdam, poked fun at the citizens of Amsterdam for living in trees, like rooks, because their houses were all set on piles.)

Amsterdam is famous for its fine Jewry, and there are ten synagogues. Rembrandt found some of his most famous models among the Jewish population. Many of the Sephardim, Portuguese and Spanish refugees, came to Amsterdam, as did Germans and Russians fleeing persecution in their own countries. Baruch Spinoza, born in Amsterdam in 1632, was the son of Portuguese Jews. The city is still the world's headquarters for diamond cutting, an art which for centuries was the preserve of these Portuguese craftsmen. Most of the mills are still owned by their descendants.

84

The Rijksmuseum in Amsterdam is one of the great art museums of the world. It contains wonderful Carolingian relics, but, above all, the greatest collection of paintings in Holland. Here is Rembrandt's "Night Watch," painted in 1642, his "Directors of the Clothmakers Guild," and over a dozen more. Here are some of the finest canvases by VERMEER, doubly interesting for their detailed interior views of seventeenth-century Dutch houses. Here is the work of Rubens, Van Ruisdael, Brueghel, and the lusty portraits by Hals, which compete with the fine collection of this master's work at Haarlem.

Outside Amsterdam, Zaandam, with its more than four hundred windmills, consisting of oil, saw, corn, paint, cement and paper mills, is an astonishing sight. Windmills, many of huge dimensions, some with each sail more than sixty feet long, are not folksy conventions but are essential to the Dutch economy. They are also used, most importantly, to pump superfluous water from the low ground to the canals which empty it into the sea. Since the terrible breakthrough of the spring of 1953 even more windmills have been set up everywhere.

Northeast of Amsterdam are those quaint little fishing villages of Marken and VOLENDAM. Here the natives dress up in their antique costumes, day in, day out, year in, year out, and mainly exist, it would seem, for the benefit of tourists. Unselfconscious, they behave prettily and unaffectedly with the unconcern of goldfish in a goldfish bowl. The costumes worn are those of the sixteenth and seventeenth centuries, the ages of the great painters.

ALKMAAR is the center of the cheese industry, and the Friday markets are frequented by buyers from all over the country, who get the cheeses here direct from the makers. Over ten thousand tons of cheese are weighed annually in the town WEIGHING HOUSE, built in 1582. The huge piles of produce make a brave sight, and the popular Dutch custom of eating cheese at breakfast has much to recommend it. Aalsmeer, near the Schiphol airport, is made up of green islands that grow nothing but flowers; these are gathered and sold at the largest daily flower auction in the world, and are sent by air all over Europe, and some across the Atlantic.

The once flourishing port of ENKHUIZEN in North Holland, now a railway terminus and fishing and shipbuilding center, still has many architectural reminders of a vigorous past. The 1540 DROMEDARY overlooking the harbor is but one of several old gateways which still stand; the ancient assembly house of the dike reeves of Holland and West Friesland is here, and the weighing house, built in 1559. Worshipers gather before the beautifully carved Renaissance screen and sixteenth-century pulpit in the Westerkerk, with its quaint 1519 wooden bell house, or in the Zuiderkerk. The Town Hall, old mint, and orphanage are all seventeenth century. Interesting, too, is the Zuider Zee Museum which displays fascinating scale models of the great land reclamation project.

Utrecht, on the Oude Rijn, with a university and cathedral, contains also the Royal Mint and the Maliebaan, a triple avenue of lime trees, spared by the Roi Soleil, Louis XIV. Hilversum is also full of excellent modern buildings, including the Town Hall designed by Dudok.

Many of the splendid old castles in Holland have been turned into museums, filled with period furniture, and are open to the public all the time. Others, still in private hands, are usually open on specific days. Cannenberg, Middachten, Ruurlo are all well worth visiting.

Near Arnhem and Otterlo, in a national park of 14,000 acres once belonging to the Kroller-Muller family, is the Van Gogh museum with 270 of his paintings, drawings, and water colors. It is a most perfectly designed modern picture gallery, built by Van de Velde, completely functional and in flawless taste—fitting, or rather folding, into the landscape to perfection. During the last war Field Marshal Goering made off with some of the early Flemish primitives which the museum also contains, having long cast covetous eyes at the paintings. It took quite a time to get them back.

Holland is basically pastoral, a farming country whose cities are markets to which the farmers come with their wares. And just as essentially Holland is mercantile, a country whose chief friend and chief foe is the sea: friend upon which one sails to conquer or to trade, to fish or to ferry; foe which destroys in a few hours the work of centuries, whose waters bring death, not life, which is never wholly at peace nor is ever tamed.

But Holland, which has one of the lowest illiteracy rates in the world—2 per cent—and probably the highest longevity average in Europe—seventy-one years—is also highly industrialized. About 40 per cent of the population is employed in a variety of industries, of which by-products from the coal industry, oil (Holland has an oil field in Schoonebeek which supplies 30 per cent of the domestic consumption and, at Pernis, the largest oil cracking installation in Europe), shipbuilding, and metal are the most notable. Holland also produces 45 per cent of the world production of condensed milk.

The standard of living in Holland is one of the highest in Europe today. Rationing is a thing of the past; new buildings have been put up and in some cases whole villages and towns have been rebuilt since the war and since the floods of 1953. The Dutch motto, *Je maintiendrai,* "I will preserve," is as appropriate today as ever it was.

DENMARK

The whole of Denmark is about half the size of Maine, and there are only just over four million Danes in the world—not very much more than the population of Chicago. Denmark consists of the peninsula of Jutland, with 150 people to the square mile, and of some 500 islands, only 100 of which are large enough to be inhabited, with around 400 people to the square mile. Denmark grows four times as much as the population requires for food, yet 60 per cent of the people live in towns, and 20 per cent more persons are now employed in industry

and handicrafts than in agriculture, horticulture, and forestry combined.

Copenhagen, the capital, holding over a quarter of the population, is the gayest city of northern Europe. It is often called "the Paris of the north"; the night life is extensive and inexpensive.

Because of the Gulf Stream the Danish climate is mild. There is marvelous swimming in the summer, little snow in winter, and from April to November the weather is glorious. Almost everyone sails, for eighty of the Danish cities and towns are on the sea or on some bay, and water surrounds all the land except the narrow neck of South Jutland where Denmark is joined to Germany.

Denmark has no natural resources beyond its farms and fish—and its people. There is not a single mine; no iron, copper, tin, oil, coal; no "forests for pulpwoods, not even a waterfall to generate cheap electric power, no colonies from which to commandeer commodities." The Danes have to import all raw materials for their industries except lime for cement—and all that their possession, the huge island of Greenland, produces is cryolite. Yet their metal industry is one of their largest.

Norwegian novelist Sigrid Undset (born in Denmark) declared the Danes to be "an unmilitary, but fiercely courageous people." Their total of over three thousand who died in the resistance during the German occupation, and six hundred more who died in concentration camps, is impressive, as was the heroic gesture of the thirty-six young men of the Royal Life Guards, in their sky-blue trousers and towering bearskin helmets, who, in 1940 when the first armored German troops entered the Palace square, leveled rifles, took aim, and fired.

Denmark is the oldest monarchy in Europe, and since Gorm the Old, who came to the throne around 883, the Danish kings have ruled and reigned over Denmark. But not over Denmark only. In 1028 Canute the Great ruled England and Norway too (the Faeroe Islands, north of Scotland, which still are Danish, are a lasting memorial of that conquest). By 1241, under Waldemar the

Victorious, Estonia, Holstein, Pomerania and parts of Prussia were Danish. Under Margaret, daughter of another Waldemar (she died in 1412), the three kingdoms of Norway, Denmark and Sweden were united, while Finland and great stretches of the Baltic were also under Margaret's wise sway. Yet the Danish kings have always acknowledged higher authority: all the way from Canute, who teased and taught his flattering courtiers, to Waldemar the Victorious who declared "By Law shall the Land be built" and to Waldemar IV (1320-1375), who stated, in answer to papal pretensions, "our nature we have from God, our rule from our people, our abilities from our forefathers, and our throne from our foregoers—from you we have nothing and to you we give nothing." From these on down to the present democratic and popular King Frederick IX and Queen Ingrid, under whom 95 per cent of Danish farmers own their land and 90 per cent of all the people are insured against sickness, and 100 per cent against old age, the record is extraordinary.

COPENHAGEN, founded by Bishop Absalon in 1167, is one of Europe's busiest ports. By air it is only a few hours from Paris or London, by ship about nine days from New York, and is easily reached from most cities in Europe. The first thing one notices on arrival in Copenhagen are the bicycles which "flow through the streets like freshets." Surely even in Holland there are not so many! Karel Capek said that in Copenhagen the bicycle is no longer a means of transport but "has become something like a universal element along with earth, water, fire and air."

Town Hall Square is the center of the city, dominated by a green-spired tower 350 feet high. Dr. Hudson Strode, who has written admirably about Denmark and knows it well, declares the "tone" of Copenhagen to have been set around 1600 by King Christian IV, a jolly monarch, with twenty-two children, natural and legitimate, and a genius for building and planning. The Town Hall Square is linked with the King's New Market by a mile-long series of five narrow streets known collectively as Stroget (Main Street).

Here are the showrooms of the Royal Copenhagen porcelain, and Georg Jensen's famous silver. Indeed, Copenhagen is among the world's best shopping centers, furs, toys, ceramics, and handwork being especially good buys. It's also one of the best places in the world to eat, and the drink, whether coffee, snaps or *akvavit,* cherry brandy, or beer, is excellent.

The lovely Stock Exchange, with its spire topped by four copper dragons standing on their heads with tails entwined, is, of course, due to Christian IV, and has been in use since 1640. The Round Tower, once an astronomical observatory, is of brick with double windows in perpendicular rows nine stories high. No stairs go up—but a spiral causeway broad enough to take a carriage and pair through (Peter the Great drove up in one). Charlottenborg Palace, granted by Frederick V to the Academy of Arts, is near the NYHAVN, along the right bank of which (contrasting with Paris' Left) live artists, actors, dancers, and their camp followers, in delightful old gabled houses.

Nyboder, a series of "charming, low yellow houses arranged on neatly patterned streets," was built by Christian IV for his sailors, and here now are the homes of both active and retired navy men. AMALIENBORG SQUARE, enclosed by four almost identical rococo PALACES built between 1750 and 1760, is one of the loveliest architectural units anywhere in the world. Here is the official residence of the king and queen. And here, in this gloriously symmetrical square, the Changing of the Guard occurs daily at noon.

Copenhagen is full of CANALS and a delightful way to see the city is to take one of the many little motor boats moored for hire. Here the principal idea of the canals is to bring the sea into as close an association as possible with the daily life of a city which owes to it all its prosperity and much of its food. (Quite the opposite from Holland, where it is the land that is precious, and the canals are principally used to keep *out* the sea, to hold it at dikes-length.) The National Museum, which is housed in the Prinsens Palais, along the Frederiksholms Canal near

Christiansborg Palace, contains a wonderful prehistoric section illustrating the Viking era. Christiansborg Palace is the second rebuilding of the Palace, completed in 1928. The first one, on the site of the old Copenhagen Castle, burned (except for the Riding School and the Marble Bridge) in 1794; the second one in 1884. Rosenborg Palace, a rose-colored seventeenth-century building rising from a narrow moat in the King's Garden, is gay with copper turrets, pillars, baroque ornaments galore, and contains the Crown Jewels and other treasures of Danish kings. Around it is the oldest park in Denmark, laid out by Christian IV.

The New Carlsberg Glyptotek, founded by the brewer Carl Jacobsen, has first-rate Egyptian and French art. Of churches, the old Cathedral, or Vor Frue Kirke, has a splendid sculpture series of the Twelve Apostles by Thorvaldsen, and his Christ. Thorvaldsen (1768-1844) has a whole museum to himself; he and Hans Christian Andersen, the two foremost geniuses of nineteenth-century Denmark, were fast friends, although Andersen was the younger by forty years. Both bachelors, they often dined together, and did so on the last night of Thorvaldsen's life; Andersen has written charmingly of the great "Canova of the north."

Andersen's own Little Mermaid, sculptured in bronze by Erichsen, sits on a boulder at the shore's edge, at Langelinie, Copenhagen's favorite promenade, which follows a narrow strip of land, planted with flowering trees, between the water front and a moated park surrounding the old Citadel. Tivoli Gardens, laid out in 1843 on part of the old ramparts, consists of twenty landscaped acres of the most valuable real estate in the capital and has the statue of Lumbye, the most popular Danish composer. "Fountains play, flowers perfume the air, sailors hug their girls in public . . . old folk lounge on benches under the chestnut trees or stroll to a favorite cafe to eat strawberries and cream." Here are symphony, ballet, bands, fireworks, puppet shows, dancing, merry-go-rounds, clowns, and acrobats.

There are still around 2000 great private estates in Denmark, some of them royal palaces, such as Fredensborg, where the royal family live in the spring and fall. Others are castles, like Tranekaer on Langeland Island; Graasten, the summer residence of the king and queen; and Liselund, built in 1792 for his wife by M. Calmette, who had escaped the French Revolution. This last is a miniature chateau, one story in front and two behind where the land drops away; it is a dream place, surrounded by green lawns and a green lake with snow-white swans. Danehof at Nyborg on Fünen is where Denmark received her Magna Carta on July 29, 1282, and EGESKOV, also on the island of Fünen, built in 1554 on oak piles driven into a lake, is still inhabited and enchanting. Unhappiest event in Egeskov's long history was the confinement of a young girl, walled up in a single room by her father because of her love for a handsome peasant lad. FREDERIKSBORG PALACE, situated on three small islands in a lake, is perhaps the most glamorous of the castles. It was started in the early seventeenth century by King Christian IV, and is now the National Historical Museum.

One of the most visited places of all is Hamlet's KRONBORG CASTLE, at Elsinore. Built by King Frederick II in the sixteenth century, and restored in the seventeenth, it is of sandstone, roofed with copper. In summer there are the international open-air performances of HAMLET in the courtyard. The town of Elsinore is full of medieval buildings, including the churches of Saint Olaf and Saint Mary, which contribute to the enchanting Old World atmosphere.

A tour through Denmark will also take you through Köge outside which is Fjenneslev Church whose twin towers, legend has it, were built by Asser Rig's wife after giving birth to twin sons, one of whom was Absalon, who became bishop and founder of Copenhagen. From Korsör the ferry takes you to Nyborg, which is only a short distance from ODENSE, provincial capital in the heart of "the fairy island of Fyn." Odense, where Saint Canute's shrine attracted hordes of pilgrims in the Middle Ages, has a fine Gothic cathedral dedicated to him, where Kings John and Christian II also lie buried. ANDERSEN'S BIRTHPLACE is a single room in a corner house where, on a bunk made from discarded boards from a nobleman's bier, the storyteller was born on April 2, 1805. While in Odense you are also certain to see the KING'S GARDEN, bordering the eighteenth century ODENSE MANSION. Despite its age, this is a go-ahead city with textile manufacturing, sugar refining, and distillers. Across the island is FAABORG, a lovely old walled town, approached through undulating farm country, boulder-strewn hills, and beechwoods.

Jutland, which "turns its back" on the North Sea, has the lovely lake district centering around Silkeborg. AARHUS, six hours by train or overnight by boat from Copenhagen, is a delightful mixture of the old and the new. This second largest city and seaport, gay with night clubs, has an ultramodern Town Hall, finished in 1942, an even more functional university, contrasting with Marselisborg Palace, or the Gothic Cathedral of Saint Clemens, started in 1201, or the Old Town. Here the Open-Air Museum, numbering forty-eight buildings, shows the condition of Danish citizens, their houses, trade, and work for over three hundred years. Ebeltoft, Mariager, and thousand-year-old RIBE with its storks and gossip-mirrors (two-faced tiny mirrors set about a foot from the casement center so the inhabitants can watch everything that goes on in the street) are among the other lovely old places to be visited.

But for all its long history Denmark is among the least archaic of countries. Perhaps the best way to see it is to take one of the new "lifeseeing tours" which feature the modern social welfare institutions, schools, old peoples' homes, hospitals, model farms, and such engineering triumphs as the Storström bridge, Europe's longest, linking Zealand to Falster. For Denmark, as Ruth Bryan Rohde, former American Minister to Denmark put it, "has a mission in world reconstruction by reason of its achievement in popular democratic and social culture."

"What a noble animal is man," mused Denmark's Hamlet, and in Hamlet's country one is quite prepared to agree with him.

NORWAY

"The past is yours forever," wrote Ibsen, but the lively and charming Norwegians live very much in the present. The land of the Vikings is glorious, long, and rangy; it stretches from the comparative warmth of the North Sea to above the Arctic Circle. Where the landscape of Denmark is mild, sunny, and gay, Norway is beautiful and serious, a rugged country of extreme grandeur, with a population whose physical energy is probably at the maximum achieved by man. In the north it is almost continuously daylight from April to August; and even in the extreme south the long twilight, during the same period, brings no real darkness. In winter, the situation reverses, with light for only a few midday hours. It has frequently been said that culturally the Norwegians tend to lean toward England in the same way that the Danes look toward France, the Swedes toward Germany. There are around 3¼ million Norwegians—barely more than there are Parisians, fewer than there are Chicagoans, and the area of Norway, only four per cent cultivated, is 124,-710 square miles—less than the size of California, Texas, or Montana. Fishing and shipping are still profitable activities in Norway (Stavanger, the sardine capital, alone cans 600 million brisling a year) but no longer rank first as a means of livelihood. Norway's largest industrial concern, Norsk Hydro, produces over one million tons of nitrate fertilizers a year, made from ammonia extracted from air and water. Grea, a raw material for plastic, is another postwar development, and the Norwegian forests, occupying 24 per cent of the land, are of course immensely valuable. In 1950, 22 million, in 1952, 40 million, trees were planted with the help of the government. The swift rivers are used for the gravity carriage of timber as well as for vast hydroelectric power schemes.

Norway has produced many great men such as Edvard Grieg the composer, Ole Bornemann Bull the violinist, Henrik Ibsen the playwright, Björnstjerne Björnson the writer, Sigrid Undset the novelist, Nansen and Amundsen the distinguished explorers.

Norwegian costumes are among the most elaborate and beautiful in the world, their BRIDAL COSTUMES and ornaments are unique. The bride wears a gilt crown, filigree brooches, belts and ribbons; and the groom wears heirloom buttons and buckles. The crafts, textiles, embroideries, silver, and brassware are all first rate, and the furs are marvelous. The word "ski" is Norwegian and Norway still makes the best skis in the world. Skiing there of course is magnificent; so is skating and bobsledding. The early spring season is particularly recommended for skiing. Almost everywhere in Norway there seems to be good fishing (salmon, trout, pike), good shooting (game birds, deer, elk), good sailing and swimming.

Norwegians have always been great travelers: in the chivalrous twelfth century Sigurd Jorsalfar, a crusader, made a pompous entry into Constantinople, where he presented the Byzantine emperor with his richly adorned ships. His horse was shod with gold horseshoes; one (perhaps purposely loose!) fell off, and the honest finder was allowed to keep it. In the twentieth century Thor Heyerdahl traveled on a raft with five companions 4300 miles across the South Pacific to prove that the Polynesian islands could have been settled from Peru, and his account of the journey, *Kon-Tiki,* published in Norwegian in 1948, has been a best-seller in about a dozen languages since then. The documentary film of the adventure was released a year or two later.

OSLO, Norway's capital, which celebrated its nine hundredth anniversary with suitable splendor in 1950, has a lively and effervescent population of less than half a million. However, in 1948 it incorporated neighboring municipalities with large forest territories, and the total area of 174 square miles now makes it one of the largest cities in the world. The geographical center of Oslo today is a woodland lake far from the center of town. Oslo was founded by King Harald Haardraade, and soon boasted six churches and three monasteries. Its heyday was from 1300 to 1319, in the reign of King Haakon V, who, on the peninsula in the harbor, built the AKERSHUS FORTRESS which is still one of Oslo's landmarks. After the Reformation, the town's prosperity declined, until King Christian IV of Denmark rebuilt it in the seventeenth century, and renamed it Christiania, after himself. But in 1924-1925 it became Oslo again. The royal family, which conforms to the state religion, Evangelical Lutheran, has lived there since 1905.

Oslo is the home port for more than 40 per cent of the Norwegian merchant fleet, now third largest in the world, and is also the main traffic center of Norway. Oslo University, with nearly 4000 students, founded in 1811, is the biggest in the country. Oslo's main tree-lined thoroughfare, Karl Johansgate, is the favorite promenade: here are the Parliament Building and the Royal Palace, the university, the National Theater, with statues of Ibsen and Björnson, the Grand Hotel, leading banks, business houses, and gay cafés open far into the night. There are both medieval and ultramodern sections of the city, and the Akershus Fortress is in wonderful contrast to the Franklin Roosevelt statue, or the Fram House, where the polar exploration ship of Nansen and Amundsen is kept fully rigged. The new, red brick CITY HALL, which faces the HARBOR, is modern Oslo's pride. The Kon-Tiki Museum with Heyerdahl's raft, and the Norwegian Folk Museum, with 140 reassembled wooden buildings—including the stave church (of Gol), Ibsen's workroom, and a complete eighteenth-century Norwegian town—are all fascinating.

In Oslo's Frogner Park is the controversial "sculptural lay-out" covering 75 acres, created over a period of more than thirty years, and at vast expense, by the late sculptor, Gustav Vigeland. It is both unique and fabulous. A world of human and animal figures in stone, iron, wood, and bronze is arranged in 150 large organic groups: the monumental wrought-iron gates, with motifs from the reptile world; a bridge, with 58 bronze groups of globular-shaped humans, banked by four reptilic groups in granite; a children's playground encircled by nine bronze figures showing the child from embryo to toddler; a fountain of 60 relief and

23 tree groups, showing the life cycle; a labyrinth; a mosaic around the fountain; the monolith, a 60-foot-high granite obelisk; and a life-wheel. Horace Sutton, unkindly, describes the monolith as "carved with 121 figures hopelessly entangled in a mad scramble to reach the top. Surrounding it are thirty-six immense granite groups which were designed to represent emotions and situations from daily life. . . . The sheer volume is enough to glut the artistic sensibilities of the average tripper."

Oslo is surrounded by mountains, and a trip up to Holmenkollen, most famous of ski jumps, affords a staggering view of the city and harbor. Other good views are from the Ekeberg and the lava hills of Kolsaas.

The FIORDS are as characteristic of Norway as the Alps are of Switzerland. They fringe the whole western shoreline; many are a mile deep and a mile high. There are wonderful steamer excursions up the west coast which will take visitors to many of them. Among the best known fiords are the Hardanger, which can be reached either from Bergen or Stavanger by boat; the Fjaerland fiord, nearly twenty miles long, with a background of snow and ice; the Nord fiord, near OLDEN, which runs parallel with the SOGNE FIORD and which offers as overwhelming a combination of vast expanses of water with mighty mountains and glaciers as can be found anywhere in the world. Near here is a famous medieval STAVE CHURCH. Then there is Jöring fiord, flanked by ranges and pointed peaks, with snow and glaciers on their summits; beautiful STOR FIORD; and SALT FIORD, which is near Bodö. GEIRANGER FIORD is notable for its sheer cliffs, numerous waterfalls, and mountain scenery, including SAATHORN, which rises 5835 feet at its side. Here the Seven Sisters Waterfall tumbles down a perpendicular cliff, as does the Bridal Veil, one of the most nearly perfect falls imaginable.

On the tableland are the highest peaks in Norway, the Glittertind and the Galdhöpiggen, both over 8000 feet. Three of the largest lakes, Bygdin, Tyin, and Gjende, are at more than 3000 feet, and there are numbers of small ones. There is magnificent climbing in this region, though for the most part guides are necessary. There are excellent, inexpensive accommodations everywhere, for "a Norwegian who can walk can ski," and since in summer climbing is popular, most of the ski huts are kept open, serving a double purpose, summer and winter. The Jostedalsbreen, with glaciers running from it, is the greatest ice field in Europe; it is some 1600 feet thick and over 400 square miles in area. At the Arctic Circle, too, near the coast is the great ice field of SVARTISEN.

BERGEN, founded in the eleventh century by King Olaf, is the second city of Norway; it has now around 114,000 people. Bergen was the birthplace of Edvard Grieg; and his home, Trollhaugen, in the suburb of Hop "sits in a grove of white birches with purple pansies and scarlet geraniums all around." Ole Bull, the famous violinist (one of his souvenirs in Bergen is a violin with a woman's head for a scroll, another is a program from a "farewell tour" concert at Buffalo, New York, in 1853), discovered Grieg and was the founder, amidst considerable financial trouble, of Bergen's National Stage in 1850. Later, both Henrik Ibsen and Björnson were directors of the theater, raising the drama to its pre-eminent position in their city. Bergen has a yearly music and drama festival in June. Protected from the mainland by seven mountains, the city has a moist, mild climate, and the people are especially sociable and lively.

Bergen is also the fishing center of Norway, and the town's prosperity is based on shipping cod-liver oil, herrings, and sardines. Near the harbor, with its enormous fish market, is a medieval quarter with white frame houses; and the Hanseatic Museum is full of relics of the time when Bergen was one of the greatest of Hanseatic League towns. The oldest building is the Maria Kirken, and the twelfth-century Cathedral is a rather fruity version of Gothic. Near Bergen are many of the unique stave churches, often situated in a deep valley flanked by giant peaks or on some headland overlooking a fiord. E. R. Yarham, in the *American-Scandinavian Review,* has described them:

"Built with massive timbers, now black

with age, and many of them grotesquely carved, they . . . are made throughout of pine, or other soft wood, and their scaly appearance, as of some prehistoric or oriental monster, is due to the whole of their exterior being covered with small pointed shingles, which have been preserved by the frequent application of pitch. This, and the mellowing of age, gives them their rich, brown color, and their gables grouped to a pyramid, and each surmounted by a dragon-like head seeming to spit forth flame, further enhance their fantastic aspect. At one time there were about three hundred, but today hardly a score survive. . . . They are not only pagoda-like but resemble the old Viking longships. . . . The church at Heddal, for instance, the largest of its kind, built during the thirteenth century, gives the impression of a great broad beamed boat."

The Borgund church, dating from around 1200, has been beautifully restored and has a nave and aisles with twelve columns, and a choir with a semicircular apse. When the doors are closed, the only light admitted is by small openings in the walls, for window glass was unknown in medieval Norway.

In Bergen, the Flöien funicular should be taken; it goes 1050 feet above the town, taking only ten minutes, and both the view and the restaurants on top are excellent. The Oslo-Bergen railroad is a miracle of engineering and one of the most scenic anywhere. The train goes up over 4000 feet, through 184 tunnels and under 10 miles of snow sheds. If you stop off en route at Myrdal, already some 3000 feet up, the spur line can be taken to Flaam, getting you there inside the hour. The Flaam line, crossing devious waterfalls, at one point is forced to make a complete loop inside a mountain. After the crashing, violent railway trip, as Horace Sutton wrote, "Flaam is a sudden enclave of serenity, sitting there at the edge of its waterfront with the hulking canyon walls all around."

Trondheim, in the north-central region, the third largest city, founded by King Olaf Tryggvesson, has the grandest church in Norway. Begun in the eleventh century, it became the place of burial, later the coronation church of the Norwegian monarchy. Bluish soapstone and Almenningen marble are used decoratively in early Gothic style, intermingled with Romanesque. There are also four lovely bridges over the river Nid. Trondheim was one of the first cities attacked by the Germans in 1940, and was the center of heroic resistance against overwhelming odds. Trondheim is also the gateway to northern Norway where the midnight sun is visible from May 16 to July 29, and all around the city is good sailing and skiing. The delightful ski lodges, as all over Norway, provide simple and gay hospitality.

The modern poet, S. Wolff, writes: "Glorious is my native land, the ancient cliff-bound Norway, with summer valley and winter fastness. Even if the globe were shaken, the storm would be unable to overthrow its mountains."

SWEDEN

While traveling in Sweden, it is easy to forget that these people, among the most highly civilized, socially conscious, and practically artistic in the world, whose armed neutrality is as vital as most nations' belligerency, were for centuries pirates and raiders, who terrorized Ireland, Germany, Russia, France, and even Constantinople. The Swedes penetrated far into Russia, and Poland was long a Swedish satellite. These descendants of the Vikings today are the poachers-turned-gamekeepers of Europe, even as Nobel, the giver of the Peace Prize, was one of the biggest munitions makers of Europe.

Sweden has integrated industry with the good life, and, above all, with the beautiful life, in a unique way. All its cities are happy mixtures of ancient and modern; its craftsmanship, whether in silver, steel, glass, iron, china, wood, or textiles, is always in excellent taste, but also admirably functional. Nothing we see from Sweden is amateurish or arty-crafty, shoddy or unpractical.

Sweden—with its 173,349 square miles, half-covered by forest, 30 per cent by mountains and lakes, and a tenth by water, leaving a tenth for agriculture—forms the eastern side of the Scandinavian peninsula and is about twice the size of Minnesota. The population is nearly seven and a quarter million, roughly that of New York. Around 775,000 live in STOCKHOLM, its capital, one of the most beautiful cities in the world, noble and massive, "luminous everywhere with the light reflected in the ever present water of its canals and lakes." The CITY HALL, Stockholm's trade mark, is a model of civic architecture. From the Norrbro, the bridge with seven granite arches, is the view of which the Swedish poet Tegnér wrote:

Tower, heroes' statues, palace, muses' fane
Stand nobly mirrored in the stream below;
While bathed in evening red glows Riddarholm
Where, beneath marble, Sweden's glory sleeps.

The Old City contains the STORKYRKA, or Great Church, dedicated to Saint Nicholas and supposedly founded by Birger Jarl in 1264. Among its treasures is the sculptured Saint George and the Dragon and the lovely carved wooden figure of a fifteenth-century PRINCESS. The old city is also the business center, with the Stock Exchange in the Stortorg, and the Riddarhus (House of Nobles) of Dutch-French rococo style built in Queen Christina's reign, around 1641. Here, too, is the Riddarholm Church, with a 295-foot cast-iron spire, where Sweden's kings and heroes have been buried, mostly since the time of Gustavus Adolphus, and where paintings and trophies are housed. The Royal Palace, a great rectangular building enclosing a square court, was completed in 1754, but much restored in 1901. It is open to visitors, as is Waldmarsudde, the home of the late Prince Eugen. He was one of Sweden's most distinguished landscape painters, and also an art collector like the present king, Gustaf Adolf VI, whose collection of Chinese porcelain is one of the richest in the world. The National Museum contains works of Swedish artists of all epochs, admirable collections of Dutch seventeenth-century and French eighteenth- and nineteenth-century pieces, as well as the work of moderns. At Djurgarden, an islet close to the mainland, which King John III turned into a royal deer park in 1579, are the 1000-year-old oak trees. Here, also, are amusements in the summer and the famous Skansen open-air museum with its exhibits and buildings which illustrate life in Sweden through the centuries back to the days of the Vikings. Closely connected with Skansen is the Northern Museum with the royal armory.

Stockholm offers good food with its *akvavit*, Swedish massage with its baths, excellent hotels, and twelve legitimate theaters giving native plays and concerts and frequently New York and London hits. In 1838 the Royal Opera heard the launching of Jenny Lind, twelve years before P. T. Barnum toured her through the United States; and twentieth-century Stockholm trained Greta Garbo and Ingrid Bergman at the Royal Dramatic Theater before they took to Hollywood and celluloid.

Drottningholm, the king's summer palace on an island in Lake Mälaren, is under an hour from Stockholm by one of the little white steamers. Built by Nicodemus Tessin for the widow of Charles Gustavus in the seventeenth century, it has been called the Swedish Versailles, but is, to say the least, of a more practical size. The formal French garden is full of bronze statues, and there is a Chinese pagoda in the park, erected in 1770. Here too is the enchanting Drottningholm Court Theater, established in 1769 and carefully preserved. Every summer, performances are given in eighteenth-century settings. Original stage machinery and decorations are used, while the performers are wigged and dressed just like the original performers nearly two hundred years ago.

GRIPSHOLM, about three hours from Stockholm by boat, is a splendid sixteenth-century palace (built in 1537 by Gustavus Vasa), with four red towers, looking down into the Mälaren; which forms a moat. Inside are nearly two thousand portraits of kings and notables, as well as lovely ceilings, furniture, and tapestries.

In Uppland, about twenty miles north of

Stockholm, are the churches of Harncvi and TABY, which Albertus Pictor decorated between 1470 and 1490. The medieval Swedish artist did paintings in twenty such churches, but the murals in these two are the best preserved and are completely magnificent.

Uppsala, forty miles north of the nation's capital, is the seat of the archbishop. The Cathedral, begun in 1287, was restored in the 1890's. Uppsala has a fifteenth-century university where, in 1724, the great Swedish scientist, philosopher, and mystic, Emanuel Swedenborg politely declined the chair of mathematics on the pretext that it was "a mistake for mathematicians to be limited to theory." The university library, with half a million books, contains many rare manuscripts, including the Gothic Four Gospels translated by Bishop Ulfilas in the second half of the fourth century. Uppsala's historic castle, founded in 1548 by Gustavus I, has been partially restored since the fire of 1702. It was here that Queen Christina abdicated in favor of Charles X before she sailed for Rome to spend the rest of her days in Italy.

The province of Södermanland, dotted with countless lakes, is popularly said to be where the Creator "forgot to separate land from water." On Lake Valdemaren is the castle of Prince Wilhelm, and on the shore of Lake Mälaren are many castles of the seventeenth and eighteenth centuries. The main target of the Stockholm resident in summer, however, is the Stockholm archipelago which offers good sailing and swimming off the islands.

KALMAR, on the strait between the mainland and Oland, is the site of the formation of the Kalmar Union of 1397, when Eric of Pomerania was elected king of all three Scandinavian countries. Its castle, "Key to Sweden," is a large square building with ramparts, moats, and five towers, dating from the twelfth century. The inlaid paneling in the royal chamber is particularly magnificent, so is the Renaissance fountain in the court.

VISBY, the capital of Gotland, the largest island in the Baltic, was one of the Hanseatic towns, on the prehistoric trade route via Novgorod to Asia. In the thirteenth century the town was so rich that it was said its inhabitants weighed gold with twenty-pound weights, while their pigs ate out of silver troughs and their women spun with golden distaffs. However, in 1293 the Hanseatic League declared that appeals from the factory at Novgorod should no longer be heard at Visby, but at Lübeck, and from then on Visby declined in importance, although it is still a fascinating town.

Situated at the foot of a 132-foot cliff, the *klint,* Visby still has its town walls, with 60-foot towers, while between them a series of bartizans stand on the wall, supported by corbels outside. There are traces of four parallel moats. Visby, now popularly termed the "Town of Ruins and Roses," is full of ruined churches, of which Saint Nicholas', with two rose windows still extant, is the most important.

Malmö is the capital of the chateau province of Malmöhus, the richest, southernmost, and most populated part of the country. Here are no mountains, but instead rolling hills and fertile farm areas. The white, half-timbered houses, reaching along straight avenues of willows, are characteristic of the nation's granary. Malmö has excellent modern buildings, and some good Renaissance houses. The castles of Vittskövle, Glimmingehus, Oveds Kloster, Sofdeborg, and Trolleholm, in this region, are splendid. Lund, a medieval city that once was an archbishopric with twenty-three churches, has a late-Romanesque Cathedral and a university, with fine avenues of chestnut, elm, and lime. The students wear white velvet caps, edged with blue.

Sweden's second biggest city, Göteborg (Gothenburg), is a thriving modern port on the west coast. This part of the country, along the Skagerrak coast, is reminiscent of Maine. The best seamen hail from here, and villages like Marstrand, MOLLÖSUND, Smögen, and Fjällbacka along the ragged, rocky coastline earn their bread by fishing and attract summer visitors in droves. Göteborg is the western terminus of the Göta Canal route, through Sweden's lake district to the nation's capital. The route follows the Göta River from Göteborg to Lake Vänern, the country's largest lake, which is south of Värmland, a province of lakes and forests. To the east of Lake Vänern lies the Kinnekulle, a slate mountain with bold cliffs and rich vegetation. On its slopes are old manors, such as Hällekis, with a lovely park, Rabäck, Blomberg, and Husaby, the last two with eleventh-century churches.

DALECARLIA, Sweden's oldest industrial center, is famed for its copper mines which are now nearly exhausted. The great wealth of the Falun mine contributed much to Sweden's powerful international position in the sixteenth and seventeenth centuries. Dalecarlia is also an important ski center and the Vasa Ski Race over a distance of fifty-five miles is held here every year. Here is the clear blue lake country with woodlands, pastures, hills, and mountains. Native villagers wear traditional dress on Sundays, and local music and midsummer dance festivals keep alive the color and revelry of the past.

In HELSINGLAND the unique architecture is one of the chief attractions. The timbered onion domes of belfries, separate from the churches, are very characteristic. Equally popular and with invigorating air and lovely scenery is mountainous Jämtland. Ostersund, the provincial capital, has good hotels and offers excellent skiing nearby.

Lapland, Sweden's largest and northernmost province, lies nearly six hundred miles north of Stockholm, but can be comfortably reached from there by train. Its vast expanses of unspoiled natural beauty, its majestic mountains, and, north of the Arctic Circle, the ethereal midnight sun (from May to July) are a thrilling experience. Kiruna is a modern industrial town with immense open-pit iron mines, on the same latitude as northern Alaska. The most magnificent scenery, perhaps, is in the Lake Torne Träsk region, where the summer temperature often rises to 85 degrees. Here is Riksgränsen, a fine resort, as well as Abisko and Björkliden. Lapland is full of strange natural formations, dramatic glacial peaks, lakes, and the great rushing rivers which rise in this glistening land of the hospitable nomadic Lapps and their invaluable reindeer.

FINLAND

Finland, fifth largest country in Europe and with more woods and lakes in proportion to its size than any country in the world, occupies 130,165 square miles. Surrounded by Norway and Sweden on the west and Russia on the east its four million people belong linguistically to the Finno-Ugric family (as do the Estonians and Hungarians). Theirs is the hardest of all the European languages to learn, but many understand English, and the average traveler gets along fine.

An integral part of Sweden for over eight hundred years, Finland became a grand duchy of Russia in 1809, with its own laws, monetary unit, Senate; finally it became an independent republic in 1917. Despite World War II, this modern country's cultural and economic progress has been astonishing. The domestic, public, and industrial building, especially in and around Helsinki, is as advanced as any other country (or city) in Europe, perhaps more so.

The country itself is in general rather flat, rising in the far north to low mountains, the highest peak of which is just over 4000 feet, but it has a majestic and rugged quality which Jean Sibelius conveys so magnificently in his music.

This is the forest primeval. The murmuring
pines and the hemlocks, . . .

Longfellow was so impressed with the *Kalevala,* Finland's epic poem, that Hiawatha's song became an imitation of the great Finnish classic. Though it was sung by the minstrels and told from generation to generation, no one ever wrote down the story until the nineteenth century when Dr. Elias Lönnrot trailed from one Finnish village to the next, listening to the local storytellers, hearing the ballads, and piecing together the tale of Wainamoinen, the inventor of the sacred harp, Ilmarinen, the smith, and Lemminkainen, the gallant, heroes three whose mythical adventures keep the romantic *Kalevala* alive in the minds and hearts of the story-loving Finns.

Finland in many respects is not unlike Minnesota, but with sixty thousand lakes instead of ten thousand, and 71 per cent of the land in forest—mostly pine, spruce, white birch, and aspen. It is quite logical that 85 per cent of Finland's exports should consist of lumber and other products made of wood. (A small but very select percentage may be accounted for in the modern furniture, in excellent taste, exported to New York and other American cities, as well as to different parts of Europe.) The tremendous growth of Finland's lumber industry has taken place almost entirely since 1917. In the nineteenth century, iron and smelting were considered Finland's greatest industrial potential, but now Finland supplies one-fifth of the world's coniferous lumber, and more than one-fifth of its plywood.

HELSINKI, capital and cultural center of Finland, is set amidst beautiful scenery and is known for its attractive parks, colorful outdoor cafés, beaches, and many tempting restaurants. It is particularly noted, however, for the ultramodern architecture of its churches, public buildings, and apartments. Here the 1952 Olympic Games were appropriately held in the Olympic Stadium, built in 1939. The SUURKIRKKO CATHEDRAL is on Helsinki's principal square, near the university and the municipal buildings. SOUTH HARBOR, with its bustling market, is one of five harbors belonging to this great northern port which is closed by ice during part of the winter, but is actively open the rest of the year. In January through February, the average temperature of the capital is lower than Boston but rather higher than Chicago at the same time of year.

Two hours by train from Helsinki is fashionable Aulanko, on the shore of Lake Vanajavesi in central Finland. It can also be reached in six hours by water bus from Tampere. Aulanko, in the middle of a national park, is the number-one resort in Finland. Beautiful, and with every kind of sport and creature comfort, the world seems warm and relaxed, especially after the traditional Finnish *sauna* (steambath), which everyone should try at least once. The famous Hattula Church, built in 1250, is only a short dis-

tance from Aulanko; and ten minutes from the resort is Hämeenlinna, the birthplace of Sibelius. Tampere is the industrial center and third largest city in Finland. The Cathedral has fine frescoes, and the surrounding lakes are spectacular. So also are the Tammerkoski Rapids, which flow through the town, furnishing hydroelectric power for many of its very numerous factories.

At picturesque Savonlinna, in the eastern part of Finland, is SAINT OLAF'S CASTLE, built on an island in 1475 by Eric Axelsson. It is the finest and best preserved of the medieval Finnish castles and has three massive round towers. During the summer there are good theater and opera there. Near Joensuu, the capital of Karelia, also in the eastern part of Finland, is Koli, whose high ridges afford magnificent views over endless forests and hills, leafy-shored lakes, steep granite rocks, and deep ravines.

Rovaniemi, the capital of Finnish LAPLAND, is about four hours by air and twenty-two hours by train from Helsinki. It is located almost on the Arctic Circle. Completely destroyed in the last war, it has since been rebuilt. The Lapland country is ideal for skiing and camping and is wonderfully accessible by bus. For the convenience of the traveler there are several modern tourist inns such as those at Pallas, Kilpisjärvi, and Inari. The best season for skiing on the treeless mountain slopes and reindeer-joring (riding in a one-seated pulka) is February through April. About 2500 Lapps, the original inhabitants of Finland, dress warmly and colorfully and live chiefly on a diet of fish and reindeer meat.

The Finns are one of the most gifted of peoples, with rich poetry and wonderful folk music and dances. Such men as Sibelius, the architect Alvar Aalto, Frans Sillanpää, who won the Nobel prize for literature in 1939, Tancred Borenius, the great art expert, and Mika Waltari, the best-selling novelist, have all distinguished Finland's name in the fields of music, literature, and art. The great energy, courage, and resilience of her whole people, strongly manifest particularly in this century, have won the astonished admiration of all nations.

stich

BELGIUM

Above: Ostend. Old Harbor. The port is famous for its sea food. Dozens of restaurants line the quay.

Waterloo. Modern sidewalk café in the town renowned for the defeat of Napoleon in 1815.

Sabena

Brussels. "La Maison du Roi" (Broodhuis) facing the Hôtel de Ville in the Grande Place of the Belgian capital.

ostich

Above: The busy port of Antwerp, showing the remains of the old fortifications, now used as a maritime museum.

Right: Romanesque and Gothic buildings on the Quai aux Herbes in Ghent, capital of East Flanders.

Ewing Galloway

Sabena

Opposite: The handsome restored Château of the counts of Flanders, in Ghent, dates back to 1180.

N.N.T.

Leyden, on the Oude Rijn, native town of Rembrandt and other Dutch painters.

The Peace Palace at The Hague, used for international conferences.

Opposite: Canal and street in Delft. The town is noted for its blue-and-white faïence pottery.

Amsterdam. Canal view with old buildings and Church of Saint Nicholas.

Vermeer's "The Letter," among the great paintings in the Rijksmuseum, Amsterdam.

A corner on the Amstel River in Amsterdam. At left is Hôtel de l'Europe.

shing boats at Enkhuizen harbor, North Holland. The Dromedary (1540) is at left.

Ewing Galloway

opposite: On the paved dike at Volendam, in North Holland, adjoining Edam on the shores of the Zuider Zee.

Windmills and tulip fiel
familiar sights througho
Holland.

Alkmaar, North Hollan
center of the cheese trade.
front of the weighing hou
(1582), huge piles of chees
are stacked on market day

Kostich

Thatched roofs, timbered brick walls, and woven fences are typical of old Danish farms.

Quay of Nyhavn in the nation
capital.

Copenhagen. Amalienborg Squa
from the balcony of Christia
VII's palace.

Kostich

penhagen. Boats on the old canal. The free port played a major role in making nmark the "Emporium of Baltic trade."

Kostich

Kronborg Castle, Elsino[re], north Zealand, built [by] Frederick II, is used as [a] naval museum and for *Ha[m]let* festivals in the courtya[rd]. *Below:* Performance of [the] Shakespearean classic, w[ith] Michael Redgrave a[nd] Yvonne Mitchell.

Black S[tar]

bove: Frederiksborg Palace
n Hilleröd Sound, north
ealand, built 1602–1620 by
hristian IV. *Right:* Egeskov
astle, Fünen, is sixteenth
ntury.

The Vesterport, ancient entrance to the picturesque town of Faaborg, in southwest Fünen.

Odense, Fünen. King's Garden and Odense Mansion (1719). The city is the burial place of Canute.

John E. Carrebye

stich

The little house in Odense where Hans Christian Andersen was born.

Courtyard in a picturesque old Danish farm.

Above: Aarhus. Characteristic houses in the old town open-air museum. *Left:* Storks build nests on roofs and chimneys in 1000-year-old Ribe, south Jutland, adding to the fairy-tale atmosphere.

NORWAY

Stave Church at Sogne fiord, near Balestrand. *Below:* Oslo. The harbor and city, seen from Akershus Fortress. The new City Hall is in center.

Kostich

Ewing Gallow

Stor fiord, a small village at the foot of snow-capped mountains in Möre-Romsdal.

Country road near Olden in the western fiord country.

Opposite: Geiranger fiord, in Möre-Romsdal, with farm in foreground and Saathorn, 5835 feet, in distance.

Kostich

Kostich

Salt fiord, near Bodö in Nord-
land.

Bridal costume of the northern
fiord country.

120

Bergen. Hanseatic houses on the quay. The seaport is the birthplace of Edvard Grieg, and gateway to the western fiords.

Svartisen. Glacier and fiords at the Arctic Circle.

Kostich

Stockholm, beautifully situated at the junction of Lake Mälare
and the bays of the Baltic. General view of the Old City.

…ockholm. The City Hall, finished in …22, is the capital's prominent mod-…n landmark.

Ewing Galloway

…ripsholm Palace, with its lovely for-…al gardens, is three hours by boat …om Stockholm.

…ostich

123

Refot

S. Larson

Above: Kalmar Castle, started in the XIIth century. The town on the Baltic gives its name to the 1397 union formed by Sweden, Norway, and Denmark.

Dalecarlia, ski district, land of the midnight sun and of mountains, woods, lakes, and summer festivals.

Opposite: A lovely fifteenth-century princess in Stockholm's Storkyrka, or Great Church.

W. Boberg

Gustav Hansson

Taby Church, Uppland. "Jonah and the Whale" murals painted by Albertus Pictor 1470–1490

ollösund, Bohuslän. Fishing hamlet on the ragged
agerrak coast, popular with summer vacationists.

sby, Gotland. The Hanseatic ruins are the most im-
essive in Scandinavia. *Right:* Belfries separate from
e churches are characteristic in Helsingland.

FINLAND

Reindeer in Finnish Lapland. *Below:* Helsinki. South Harbor with City Hall and Cathedral in background. *Bottom:* Saint Olaf's Castle, at Savonlinna, east Finland.

F.N.T

Black Star

Aarne

WEST GERMANY

"Germany is the core of Europe. She stands at the center of her body, at the apex of her mind, in the innermost chambers of her conscious mind and subconscious being, the source of her most glorious music. Philosophy, science, history, technology are unthinkable without Germany." So writes Salvador de Madariaga y Rojo, and his brilliant study of the four archetypal Europeans—Hamlet, Don Quixote, Don Juan, and Faust—shows them as the fourfold foundation upon which Western man has built his house.

Western Germany reaches from the North Sea, with pleasant rolling dunes, shore resorts, and ports, to the glorious Bavarian Alps, from Lübeck to Asch, from Erfurt to Aachen (Aix-la-Chapelle). More than 50,000,000 highly industrious people live in this area of around 94,738 square miles, which is about the size of Oregon. The chief port of West Germany, HAMBURG, was the greatest of the old Hanseatic towns. Well and truly blitzed, Hamburg has made a remarkable recovery after the last war. Indeed West Germany's economic recovery is altogether staggering, showing a 156 per cent greater production figure today than in 1936. The visitor to West Germany will find a country that is once more in good physical and economic shape. Ruined cities and towns have been or still are being remodeled. Historic buildings are carefully restored wherever possible but there is an ambitious modern building program. The contrast between the very old and the ultramodern is remarkable, especially in the urban communities of the north. No rationing, restrictions, or shortages exist, and even with its war scars, so much of Germany is still a "beautiful country of infinite variety," as Mark Twain described it long ago.

HANOVER, whose rulers also became kings of England in the eighteenth century, lies south of the high Lüneburger Heath. Bremen, which, with Lübeck and Hamburg, make up the trio of north German Hanseatic ports, still has its large CITY HALL, and attractive old buildings, mostly restored. Osnabrück and Hildesheim are particularly noted for their cathedrals, and Hamelin—where "the river Weser, deep and wide, washes its walls on the Southern side"—for Browning's "Pied Piper" and the building there said to be the Rat Catcher's own house.

One of the loveliest parts of Germany lies in the Harz Mountains, of which Heine wrote so movingly. Here is the mysterious "spectre of the Brocken," where a man's own shadow is cast upon the clouds, and here are such walled cities as Quedlinburg, founded by Henry I, and GOSLAR, beloved of both Saxon and Frankish kings. The Goslar Kaiserhaus, the oldest lay building preserved in Germany, was built by Henry III (1039-1056). The old Town Hall houses interesting "antiquities," and the library of the church holds rare manuscripts, including some of Luther's.

Saint Boniface stayed at Scharzfeld in 750, and the medieval dukes of Brunswick-Grubenhagen started the fashionable "ball" at OSTERODE. The Saint Aegidius Church, rebuilt after a fire in 1578, and the charming Market Square are at the center of this health resort. There are beautiful walks, climbs, and rides all through the Harz Mountains, and many good slopes for skiing.

Westphalia is noted for the treaty of 1648 at Münster, and for its horses and hams. The Ruhr coal fields extend to the Rhineland, and other industries thrive at Dortmund and Hamm, both cities taken by the Allies in April 1945. The outlying regions are more à la carte. Near Ochtrup is the lovely Wasserburg, (water castle) of WELBERGEN, not moated, but built right in the water. This is as romantic as any castle on the Rhine, a tour of which should start at Cologne, the Roman city where Agrippa laid out his plans for a colony, and where stands the magnificent Cathedral. Bonn, where Beethoven was born and raised, makes musical instruments among many other things, and has an excellent university. No longer the sleepy old town where chickens pecked about the streets, Bonn today is the seat of the federal Chancellery, and active international nerve center of West Germany. Arabs, Indians, Egyptians, Iraqi, Americans, and Europeans, all contribute to the general bustle, and restaurants manfully try to cater to their widely differing tastes.

Across the river are the Seven Hills, where some of the best Rhineland vineyards are to be found. Rolandseck has a view over the river island to Drachenfels, the dragon rock; and around the Moselle wine district are wonderful medieval towns such as Boppard, with its fine walls and splendid castle; Bacharach, with the river-moated castle of the Counts Palatine; and Saint Goar, with its nut-tree avenue. Between Saint Goar and Ober Wesel is the echoing LORELEI ROCK, where, according to medieval saga, fierce dwarfs guarded the Nibelung treasure. The subsequent legend of the Lorelei Maiden started with Brentano's ballad of 1802. Other poets adapted the theme, and Heine wrote many verses which Liszt set to music:

> I do not know why this confronts me,
> This sadness, this echo of pain;
> A curious legend still haunts me,
> Still haunts and obsesses my brain.

The curious legend concerned the Lorelei who, in despair over an unfaithful lover, threw herself into the Rhine. Transformed into a siren, her echo lured fishermen to lingering death. "The man who sees her loses his sight, or reason, he who listens is condemned to wander with her forever." Wagner was never taken in by the Lorelei, but he took up heavily with the Nibelung dwarfs, and added Siegfried.

The Eifel is a wooded, mountainous area between the Rhine, Moselle and Ruhr valleys, with quiet, melodious scenery, and many lonely highland moors with small round lakes formed in the craters of extinct volcanoes. On one of these lakes, a Benedictine Abbey, Maria Laach, was founded in 1093 and still flourishes. Eschweiler has a famous Mater Dolorosa altar; Aachen has hot springs that the Romans loved and a cathedral where thirty-two kings and emperors were crowned. A short distance from here is MONSCHAU, on the French border. Scene of fighting through the Christmas of 1944, the town still has some lovely houses and continues its weaving industry. Koblenz

too is known to American soldiers who occupied it from 1919-1923 and by their sons who fought there victoriously in 1945. Its history has frequently been joined with that of France. After the classic conversation between Louis XVI and his duke at the fall of the Bastille, "Why this is a revolt!" and the answer, "No, Sire, it is a Revolution," Koblenz became the principal refuge of French aristocrats. Here the Moselle and the Lahn fall into the Rhine and the valley grows broader, flanked by the heights of Westerwald and the Eifel Hills.

Near Koblenz is RHENS, a delightful, small town with thirteenth-century city walls. In 1338 the association of electoral princes protested there against papal claims to confirm the election of German kings.

Below the mouth of the Nahe, the Rhine has to force its way through a massif of rock. Probably nowhere else are there so many castles, every hilltop sprouts one; every valley has a walled medieval city. In spring the country is a foam of fruit blossom, in the fall the vineyards are aflame and the wine harvest brings out all the ancient customs and gaiety of the Rhine Valley.

FRANKFURT ON MAIN was first mentioned in the historical records of the year 753; it now has over half a million inhabitants. Ever since medieval times, the annual fairs have attracted merchants and traders from all over Europe, and the city is still a very active manufacturing as well as an art and literary center. Here the first election of a German emperor took place in 1147, and here in 1848-1849 the first meetings of the German National Assembly were held. Saint Paul's Church was restored and rededicated in 1948; the RÖMER (old Town Hall), in which the German kings were once elected, is newly restored and the old Cathedral still stands. The house where Goethe's parents lived, and where the poet spent the years 1749 to 1765, was accurately rebuilt in 1944. The room where he was born, and all the others with the authentic furnishings, utensils, and crockery, are still shown to over 112,000 people each year. The wonderful Frankfurt art museums, galleries, and the library also have notable treasures, including superlative master oil paintings, shell and coin collections, and two Gutenberg Bibles. In contrast to the old city are the modern buildings, and Frankfurt proudly boasts the first self-service supermarket in Germany.

From Gutenberg on up, the Germans, among their long list of great scientific and industrial achievements, have always been noted for their printing, engraving, papermaking, and bookmaking. South of Frankfurt, Stuttgart scrambled to its feet after the war to maintain its position as a leading publishing center. There are lovely places to visit in Württemberg, and KIRCHHEIM on the Teck with its 1724 hall and other lovely buildings is typical of many. Here and in Baden and Bavaria, the German cities, towns, and villages are strung like medieval jewels on a belt, clear across the country.

Heidelberg, in the Neckar Valley, has the oldest German university. The Old Town is between the river and the towering castle built under the Palatine Count Ludwig I (1214-1231). The summer serenades held in the courtyard are a great attraction. The Town Hall is Renaissance; the Students prison, the "Karzer," and the Palatine Museum are also well worth visiting. There is lovely hiking in the nearby Neckar Valley, and lots to drink in Heidelberg—the traditional way the students find their way home from the "pub" is by putting the ferrule of their alpenstocks into the trolley car lines! Würzburg, the university town, where the fishermen's and the Mozart festivals are separately held, is also a busy industrial center. It is full of interesting buildings, such as the Celtic church, where Saint Killian is buried, and Marienberg Castle. The Residence of the Prince-Bishops, built in 1720 by Balthasar Neumann, has outstanding murals by Tiepolo (1751). Among Neumann's other most notable buildings is the superb pilgrim church of VIERZEHNHEILIGEN in Franconia, one of the very best specimens of German baroque architecture to be found anywhere.

Another especially bright jewel is NÖRDLINGEN, an enchanting walled city which came through two battles in the Thirty Years' War and has preserved its charms ever since.

DINKELSBÜHL, surrounded by water and with city walls dating back to 928, also has fairy-tale buildings, and music and dancing each year to celebrate the 1632 liberation of the town by the Swedes who heeded the prayers of its children.

Rothenburg, with its little red-roofed houses, its narrow streets, cozily curled up inside its walls, completes a romantic trio. Here, too, one of Germany's most famous folk festivals takes place—the "Master Drink." The full festival is held in August, but the principal scene is re-enacted daily at noon. It commemorates the saving of the town from Count Tilly during the Thirty Years' War. The Count agreed not to sack Rothenburg if the burgomeister could drain at one draught a great state beaker holding four quarts of wine. The stalwart spread his feet, took a deep breath, drained the lot in one; and the town was saved amidst wild rejoicing.

Nuremberg, as well known to children for its toymaking as it is to the art world for the birth of Dürer, has staged a brave recovery since the war. The oldest and largest of the German fairs, the "Christkindles Mart," is held here. The fair is opened by a tiny figure of the Christ Child who appears on the balcony of the Church of Our Lady, accompanied by two tinsel angels.

From Nuremberg or from Bamberg it is not far to Bayreuth, the town of Richard Wagner's life and music. The annual festival lasts through July and August and is taken very seriously indeed. This is, in fact, considered *the* great musical event of the German year, and is staged in ultramodern settings by the composer's grandsons.

South through Donauwörth, which the duke of Marlborough and Louis of Baden captured in 1704, and where the Austrians were defeated by Marshal Soult in 1805, there are lovely valleys, and fantastic mountains, dark forests and great rivers, all the way to Regensburg (Ratisbon) on the Danube. South again is Augsburg, with its wealth of both seventeenth- and eighteenth-century houses and some exceedingly fine pictures by native Hans Holbein. Augsburg is also the home town of the Fugger family, merchant princes whose bathhouses, built in 1570, and town houses are in ornate high-Renaissance style. South of Augsburg is KIRCHE IN DER WIES, the Church in the Meadow, a white and gold wonder of the richest and most glorious baroque. Even on the sunniest day, to go inside is to receive an impression of yet more light.

In the midst of the Bavarian Alps, with their puffy white clouds, their sudden, dramatic thunderstorms, their fantastic peaked rocks and somber forests—country that explains baroque architecture better than a hundred textbooks—are the two royal castles of Neuschwanstein and Hohenschwangau. Hohenschwangau, perched more than a thousand feet high, was built by King Maximilian of Bavaria in 1832, and in the intimate garden is a marble fountain, crowded with nymphs and swans. NEUSCHWANSTEIN, set even higher in glorious scenery, was modeled on the castle of the Wartburg, and built 1869-1886 for King Ludwig II of Bavaria. Although Ludwig was quite mad, his passion for castles and palaces has served posterity well.

Munich, the capital of Bavaria, though terribly damaged in the war, is largely restored and still has many treasures. In this city of painters, sculptors, musicians, and scholars the full meaning of the German word "Gemütlichkeit" has always traditionally been experienced. Here is the best beer in the world, the Löwenbrau, or Lion brew. It plays a large part at the *Oktoberfest,* held for two weeks in tents on Theresa Meadow, and with much initial pomp and pageantry. The annual celebration of the marriage of the Crown Prince (later Ludwig I) to Princess Theresa of Saxony back in 1810 still starts with a bang. The burgomeister wields his wooden mallet and drives the tap into the first barrel—echoed by tapping all over the great festival grounds. Fried fish, chicken, slices of oxen cooked on spits are consumed at a great rate, and guild and crossbow marksmen in medieval garb, pageants, and all manner of attractions keep spirits foaming as the beer.

Munich is headquarters for buying BAVARIAN COSTUMES, worn by Bavarians on Sundays and holidays (by children and adults of both sexes and all classes), and Bavarian pipes. Nearby is Nymphenburg, with its castle built in 1663 with pagodas, its ruins, its first-class china factory, and its concerts all summer long.

Not far from Munich is the highest mountain in Germany, Zugspitze, 9,720 feet, where snow flies as early as October and may last as late as May, and such mountain villages as Mittenwald (famous for its violins) and Karwendel, both excellent resorts for skiing or climbing. GARMISCH-PARTENKIRCHEN, twin towns with picturesque old houses, are in the midst of the Bavarian lake district and on every traveler's list; the Barmsee, the Eibsee and the Walchensee are all close by.

OBERAMMERGAU, where the Passion Play is given every ten years, is easily reached from Munich. The village, nearly 3000 feet high, has quaint small houses covered with bright and lovely frescoes. The Passion Play is given for four months, and in 1950 over half a million visitors came. The cast consists of roughly a thousand performers, and many of the principals are wood carvers. The Christ of 1950, Anton Pressinger, was landlord of the Alte Post Inn, the Mary is now married to the town tailor, and the Magdalen, Gabrielle Gropper, works in her father's hardware store.

LINDERHOF CASTLE, also built by Ludwig II, in the 1870's (yet another is a copy of Versailles near Herrenchiemsee) is rococo style, with waterfalls, a Neptune-bridge, temples, and grotto. The world-wide renown of BERCHTESGADEN has not been impaired by the destruction of Hitler's eyrie, and nearby König See, deep green and crystal clear, is one of the loveliest of all Alpine lakes.

Special mention must be made of German spas, which are first rate and fun. There are 240 of them in all. Baden-Baden, with a casino as well as good serious music, is probably the best known, but Kissingen, Bad Nauheim near Frankfurt, and Badisch-Rheinfelden, on the Swiss frontier, near Schaffhausen, are excellent too. Near Badisch-Rheinfelden is TODTMOOS, with a lovely old pilgrimage church set high (nearly

3000 feet) in the magnificent Black Forest.

Lake Constance is the largest lake in Germany, right at the foot of the Alps. In Constance itself there are top-notch hotels, and everywhere are lovely castles, palaces, and cathedrals. MEERSBURG is no more and no less photogenic than so many other of the beautiful places with which Germany, land of music, mountains, and festivals; of toymaking; of science and great industry; of sport and enterprise, abounds.

AUSTRIA

Lake Constance is the meeting place for Germany, Austria, and Switzerland. And here, where road signs point to countries, not cities, is a most suitable introduction to Austria, for the echo of Constantine, of the Roman Empire, is heard all over Austria, the East Province. Austria is the heart, as Germany is the core, of Europe. Within its 32,360 square miles is felt most strongly the quality of *Romanitas,* that of being mellowed by Rome, as it were, of being so civilized that the result is almost frothy, volatile, like the wonderful Austrian whipped cream, *Schlagobers,* with which the coffee is topped. And though hardly anywhere is there a country *more* scenic, nor any country where one can ski better, climb better, swim better, dance better, or have a better time, yet the whole of mountainous Austria is the pleasure ground of a city, the hinterland of Vienna—crossroads of the East and West.

Austria, which suffered so much from both World Wars, is still quartered by the four Allied powers, but its scars are wonderfully healed and the country always gives the impression of being at the still center of Europe's eternal tornado. Austrians (there are some 6,611,000 of them) have a warm welcome for everyone. The inn is the center of native life, and when you stay in an Austrian inn you become a part of the company and always enjoy yourself, whether eating Wiener schnitzel, goulash, noodles,

strudel, pastry, the delicious game; or dancing after a day's skiing or climbing; or just sitting quietly over chess or cards. Everything in Austria has charm—the practical and colorful costumes; the fascinating painted houses, inns, and furniture; the copper church spires and domes, opulently curved or yielding to the onion shapes of the East; the animals, and, above all, the people, good looking, gay, infinitely courteous and sensitively tender.

VIENNA, divided into twenty-two districts, is a town of over 1,730,000 people—almost as big as Detroit. Like Paris, culturally, Vienna is essentially a feminine city. The two differ "in that Paris prefers to give form to intellectual, Vienna to emotional, raw materials," declares Salvador de Madariaga y Rojo. "Hence Paris brings forth, breeds and matures literature, while Vienna brings forth, breeds and matures music. Vienna . . . draws to herself the violence, the virile, pristine, formless force of the Balkan nations, converging on her up the Danube valley. Centuries of courtly life have polished the old city."

The Inner City, or oldest part of Vienna, which visitors know best, is surrounded by the Ringstrasse, the magnificent tree-lined boulevard that replaces the old line of fortification. The Opera House, rebuilt since the war, is at the junction of the Kaerntnerstrasse, the main shopping street, and the Opern Ring. Near the center of the inner city is Saint Stephen's Cathedral, also now restored, with its Gothic spire 450 feet high; the Stephans' Tuerm, started in 1147, and affectionately known as "der alter Steffel," stands in the Stephansplatz. Near the Hofberg, built in 1275, are the spacious Hofgarten and Volksgarten (parks). The palace contains the private apartments of Franz Josef, and houses the Imperial collections of porcelain, pictures, and other Hapsburg treasures. All the Imperial rooms can be seen, as well as the state apartments now used by the President of Austria. The treasury contains the crown of Charlemagne, his sword and Gospels, a sword of Harun al-Rashid, and many other jewels and historic objects. The National Library contains 81,-

000 papyri, over a million books, and over 34,000 manuscripts, including the original of Tasso's *Jerusalem Delivered*. In the wonderful Albertina collection are more than 50 Raphael drawings, 150 Dürers, and over 100 Rembrandts. The Imperial Spanish Riding Academy was founded in the sixteenth century by Prince Eugene of Savoy. It still possesses some of the best horses (and their well-matched riders) in the world, though these are now kept at Wels and perform at Salzburg.

The BELVEDERE PALACE in Vienna, built 1717-1724 for Prince Eugene of Savoy, is divided into the Lower and the Upper Belvedere (restored in 1892). Between them is an enchanting terraced formal garden, with shady avenues, lawns, flower beds, and fountains. Other great palaces are the Pallavicini and the Liechtenstein, with its great collection of paintings, marvelously hung.

In Vienna, music lovers flock to the opera, the Musikverein and the Konzerthaus. The spring music festival is from May to June. BEETHOVEN'S HOUSE, where he wrote the *Eroica,* is in the suburb of Grinzing; and in and around this city of music also are the houses of Wagner, Mozart, Strauss, the younger, Schubert, Haydn, Gluck, and other composers.

Outside the Austrian capital is HEILIGEN-KREUZ with its lovely monastery and baroque sculptures. And, bordering on the Russian Zone, at Enns, is one of the most famous old monasteries in the country, near the site of Roman Laureacum and on the ancient salt route across the Danube to Bohemia; Saint Florian, founded by the Benedictines, is noted, too, for its valuable manuscripts.

SALZBURG, the great festival city, with its towering HOHENSALZBURG FORTRESS, is rivaled only by Edinburgh and Athens for its setting and situation. The town is built in lovely squares, leading into each other, and is the most perfect baroque city, divided by the Salzach River, with shady promenades on both banks. Most of the city's buildings are seventeenth and eighteenth century. The Cathedral is ornate and a perfect setting for the great Mozart masses performed there. Outside, in the square, the medieval play

Everyman is given on sunlit afternoons during the Salzburg FESTIVAL, each July and August. The angelic and diabolic voices call in the sunset from tower to tower. Above all, Mozart is most gloriously performed at the Festival, and the composer's house, near the Mozarteum, holds a summer-long music school. Visitors should go up to Hohensalzburg by cable railway, for the view and good restaurants, or up the Mönchsberg, for more good food and concerts. The Nonnberg, a spur below the fortress, houses a Gothic church and the oldest occupied Benedictine nunnery. The views from the Capuzinerberg (where Mozart wrote *The Magic Flute*) and the Gaisberg, are lyrical. Three miles to the south is Hellbrunn, a 1613 palace where fountains play on Sundays, in the formal seventeenth-century gardens, and where theater is given outdoors. Leopoldskron is another lovely local palace, where open-air concerts are also scheduled. Within the UN-TERSBERG are the oldest salt mines in Europe, with terrifying descents communicating by slippery poles dropping a sheer five hundred feet or more.

Near Salzburg is the lovely Wolfgangsee, surrounded by mountains. The Schafberg, nearly 6800 feet high, looks down on the Mondsee, Abersee and Attersee. From the top can be seen the mountains and lakes of the Salzkammergut, Upper Austria, as far as the Bohemian Forest, and the Bavarian plain as far as the Chiemsee. The loveliest places in the Salzkammergut (the Austrian lake district) are Gmunden on the Traunsee, Bad Ischl, with its salt, mud, sulphur, pine, and vapor baths, and Alt Aussee, on its lake, near the breathtakingly beautiful Dachstein ice caves. Hallstatt, too, is one of the most visited spots. Inhabited since 3000 B.C., the village can be reached delightfully from Alt Aussee, crossing the lake on a steamer which provides wonderful views of the mountains and the pink and blue gabled houses. Also in this region are the Grundlsee and the Toplitzsee, lovely, wooded and remote.

Badgastein has springs which are good for gout and nerves. Kitzbühel, with the Hahnenkamm run, is one of the best ski centers, and holds international winter sport competitions. Zell-am-See, on an attractive lake, is a good center for the High Tauern ski places. The water of the Zellersee is warm, averaging 70 degrees, and there are lovely excursions to the Schmittenhoehe, and the Kaprun Valley, with its ruined castle, highly dramatic waterfall, and fine gorge.

INNSBRUCK, the capital of the Austrian Tirol, is set among the Alps at the point where the INN VALLEY is crossed by a 2000-year-old bridge, and you see the mountains at the end of the main street. The city's fountains and the Goldenes Dachl, a small Gothic balcony three stories high with a steeply pitched and gilded roof built by Emperor Maximilian so he and his court could watch the strolling players or minstrels from above, are enchanting. The latter stands at the end of the Erzherzog Friedrichstrasse, flanked with arcades, which in turn leads into the Maria Theresienstrasse. From the cobbled Stadtplatz, the Hofgasse leads to the Hofkirche, where stands the Maximilian monument. The bronze figure of the Emperor kneels on a marble sarcophagus, around which are twenty-four reliefs in marble representing events in his life. Twenty-eight bronze statues of Maximilian's legendary ancestors and contemporaries line the nave. Here, too, is the tomb of Andreas Hofer, the Austrian patriot who defied Napoleon, was shot in Mantua in 1810, and about whom one of the best-known of German songs was written.

All around Innsbruck are natives in picturesque Tyrolean costumes, up the mountains and in the little villages and towns. The city is the center of the ski traffic; from here trains start for the famous ski resorts of Igls, Obergurgl (in the Oetz Valley), and the Arlberg—Saint Anton and Saint Christoph —and numerous others, of all sizes, to suit all competences and purses. Two cable railways, up the Patscherkofel and the Hafelekar, enchant the ascending traveler as he sees the Tirol unfolding below him. From Innsbruck the Achensee, over three thousand feet high and darkly, deeply blue, should be visited, and the lovely valleys of Zillertal, with green basins in the midst of mountains,

Oetztal, and Stubaital, the latter with splendid background views of glaciers.

The western province of Vorarlberg has the Bregenz Forest and the Vorarlbergers wear their wonderfully colorful attire every day. In the far south of Austria is the province of Carinthia, one of the sunniest places in Europe. It is reached by the breathtaking Gross Glockner, High Alpine Road over which some seventy thousand foreign cars travel each year. In Carinthia, too, is the castle fortress of the Hochoesterwitz, still in the hands of its early owners, the Khevenhueller, whose collection of ancient armor is the largest in the world.

Austria is so beautiful, so easy going, so full of treasures, music, food, and sport that Americans, like others, usually exceed their vacation schedule there—but seldom their welcome.

SWITZERLAND

"Swiss history, in which the forces of nature have proceeded along a straight line, is unified and easy to survey, is beautiful, because this variety, contradictory and tending to intensest exaggerations, could only grow into an entity in man; and the Swiss, however differently the separate cantons may have developed him, carries the consciousness of all his federated landscapes in a singularly prepared and fruitful spot in an otherwise not easily penetrated mind." So wrote Rainer Maria Rilke, the German poet, who found asylum in Switzerland, as have so many other of the world's great men. Some, like Rilke, have sought refuge from themselves; others, like Voltaire and Rousseau, from their fellow men; others from the tyranny of priests, or kings, or nations (that is, from their fellow men coagulated into synonyms of power). But to each and all, escapists or refugees, the sanity and solidity, the security and simplicity of Switzerland and of the Swiss has brought safety. Europe trusts the Swiss. They are the keepers of Europe.

Swiss, in medieval costume, guard the Vatican, and "Switzers" were the guards that kept the gates of King Claudius' Palace.

Switzerland borders on France, Germany, Austria, and Italy, and the Swiss are quadri- or quinquelingual, German, French, and Italian being spoken everywhere, Romansh and English being also understood and spoken in most places. The population is around 4,700,000, the area 15,940 square miles—about twice the size of Massachusetts. Founded in 1291, Switzerland is the second oldest republic. There are twenty-two federated cantons, governed by a constitution like that of the United States. Switzerland has given the world the idea of neutrality (enunciated by a Dutchman, Grotius, but practiced first by the Swiss) and the Red Cross. The International Labor Office and the International Telecommunications Union are housed in Geneva, and the League of Nations once was.

Switzerland is a holiday wonderland; and the Swiss, regarding tourists as a natural resource, take every care of them, treating them with the greatest courtesy and consideration. Nowhere, even in America, are hotels so clean, food more universally excellent; nowhere else in the world are trains so spotless and so comfortable. All the railroads are electrified. The standard of living is high, of literacy even higher (100 per cent); in Switzerland you need lack nothing and fear nothing. The scenery is majestic, and there are activities around the clock for all. Skiing and mountain climbing of course come first, but water skiing, swimming, sailing, motor boat racing and fishing on the lakes, golf, tennis, riding, rifle shooting and trap shooting are all indulged in by natives and tourists alike.

The Swiss towns are gems, each with a special flavor, all with charm, and all set in superlative landscapes. SCHAFFHAUSEN, to the northwest of the country on the Rhine, is the German-speaking and Protestant capital of the canton of the same name. The minster is stern and plainly Romanesque; near it is the fifteenth-century bell that inspired Friedrich Schiller's "Song of the Bell" and part of Longfellow's "Golden Legend."

To the southeast, is SAINT GALLEN, a busy industrial town producing embroidered cotton goods and Swiss muslins. It contains a Benedictine abbey, founded in the eighth century on the site of the cell of Saint Gall, an Irish monk, who taught Greek to the native clergy. The Abbey Church (or Cathedral) rebuilt in 1765, is a miracle of architectural unity, and the library, one of the most famous in Europe, is rococo, with superb parquet floors. Here there still are about four hundred manuscripts mentioned in the catalogue of 823, as well as many others.

ZURICH, the largest town in Switzerland, modern in appearance and German speaking, is the center of banking, insurance, manufacturing, and commerce. Silk is its chief product, with cotton mills, iron foundries, machine tools, and watchmaking running close. Zurich spreads out on both banks of the clear waters of the Limmat, which forms the outlet of the lake; and the Glärnisch, Drusberg, Tödi, and 10,000-foot-high Kammlistock are but some of the Alps visible from the city. The Cathedral, built in the eleventh and twelfth centuries, has Charlemagne enthroned on the west tower, with gilded crown and sword, in recognition of his gifts to the church. Zurich was Zwingli's town, and there is a museum devoted to the reformer, containing autographed letters, also a Gottfried Keller room commemorating the Swiss poet who died in 1890.

BRUNNEN, on Lake Lucerne and on the Saint Gotthard railway, is one of the chief tourist centers of Switzerland. At Brunnen the south arm of Lake Lucerne, called the Lake of Uri, begins; the mountains rise suddenly; the lake narrows. High snow-clad peaks appear and, at a sharp angle which juts into the lake, rises the Mythenstein—an 85-foot-high rock, inscribed in memory of Schiller, "who could touch nothing without ennobling it" and whose masterpiece, of course, is "William Tell." The Rütli, across the lake from Brunnen, was the scene of the founding of Switzerland's independence on August 1, 1291, and to the south, Uri Rotstock, with its glacier, is magnificent.

North of Lucerne, and nearer again to

Zurich, is Baden with its mineral springs, known since Roman times; and Brugg, a quaint town with a "Black Tower" at the bridge over the Aare, of early Romanesque origin. Near here too was the Roman city of Vindonissa, and the Habsburg castle from whence the family took its name.

In the northwesternmost part of Switzerland is Basel, second largest Swiss town. Here the roads and railway lines from the west and north, from France, Belgium, Holland, and Germany, converge. Erasmus, Holbein, Calvin, and Nietzsche spent important years of their lives in this trading center of international importance. The city is famous for its bridges, which cross the Rhine, for its fine collection of Holbein paintings, and for the old minster, the site of which was once occupied by a Roman fortress.

BERN, Switzerland's capital and one of Europe's smallest, is picturesque and largely medieval. It has many handsome towers, including the famous clock tower, sixteenth-century fountains, gayly painted statues on pillars, including the romanticized one of WILLIAM TELL, delightful arcades, and a fifteenth-century Cathedral. It also has an admirable zoo, where the animals are kept in as great freedom as possible and in natural surroundings. The bear is the emblem of Bern; and the den, where bears have been kept since the Middle Ages, is a popular sight with visitors. The old minster is surrounded by open-air markets, and there are excellent restaurants, mostly with open-air terraces, and wonderful mountain views.

INTERLAKEN, a short train ride from Bern, between the lakes of Thun and Brienz, is the gateway to the snow and glacier world of the Bernese Alps. The cog-wheel railway goes up to the Jungfraujoch, the highest railway terminal in Europe. And here in an amphitheater of mountains and glaciers are the EIGER and the MÖNCH, the JUNGFRAU, the huge precipices of the Black Mönch, the steep side of the Ebenfluh, the Gletscherhorn, the Mittaghorn, the Grosshorn, the Breithorn, and almost half a dozen more of the giants. Hilaire Belloc has described them: "Up there in the sky, to which only clouds belong and birds and the last trembling colors of pure light, they stood fast and hard, not moving as do the things of the sky." The Wetterhorn, too, can be seen and climbed from Mürren, which stands 5400 feet above the Lauterbrunnen Valley. Mürren is wonderful as both a skiing and a climbing center, and there are lovely walks all around, up the Schilthorn, for example, or the Sefinen Valley.

From Spiez the railway can be taken to Frutigen, and motor service will carry the passenger through the twelve-mile valley of the Engstligen brook to ADELBODEN. The large and delightful village has first-rate winter sports and is a starting point for yet more spectacular mountain tours.

The Swiss valleys are, in their own way, as marvelous as the mountains. One of the greenest is the Simmental, with beautiful meadows and farms enclosed by pine forests. Here, in spring, are fields of white narcissi and, later, woods full of lilies of the valley and cyclamen, while higher are carpets of blue gentian. Here the beige cows, with their musical bells, feed all summer long, and the cowboys yodel to each other, exactly as movies and books say they do. The villages are always clean, the inhabitants friendly and charmingly dressed; indeed, Switzerland seems predestined to be paradise as nearly as it can be attained here below: even the insects are not as voracious as in other countries, the cold mountain nights killing off gnats and mosquitoes to a great extent. From Zweisimmen, the chief village in the upper Simmental, the Hundsrück can easily be climbed in four hours, and from the top Mont Blanc, the Bernese, Fribourg, and Vaudois Alps can all be clearly seen.

A short distance from Zweisimmen lie Saanenmöser, Saanen, and Gstaad, villages with excellent skiing; and lower, the Lake of Geneva comes into sight, as the railway descends to MONTREUX. There are several cable railways, too, up the nearby hills. Vevey, for example, is the setting for Rousseau's *Nouvelle Héloïse,* and to Mont Pèlerin above it goes a cable railway; also to Caux and to the Rochers de Naye, with an incredibly vast panorama of the Bernese Alps, the Vaudois Alps, the Valais (Grand

Combin and Dent du Midi), the Savoy Alps, and the whole lake. Montreux itself is modern, and consists mostly of hotels, but the nearby Castle of Chillon is twelfth century. It is beautifully restored and is most attractively situated right on the lake, so that had Bonnivard been able to see out of his dungeon he might have been envied rather than pitied. Francis Bonnivard, the prisoner sung by Byron, was born in 1496, and warmly defended the city of Geneva against the duke of Savoy. The duke put him in prison, but he was freed by Bernese forces in 1536.

GENEVA, the metropolis of French Switzerland and the seat of the Reformation during the time of Calvin and of the League of Nations, is one of the most international of cities. This watchmaking center of the world is full of delightful small streets, like the RUE CALVIN and the Grand Rue, the oldest, where Rousseau was born in 1712. The waterfront boulevards look across the lake to Mont Blanc and the Savoyard shore. The Rhone leaves the lake here, and the rush of glacier-green water is a sight that many poets have struggled to describe. Outside of Geneva is Coppet, a sweet village where Madame de Staël lived; her house is exactly as it was, with wonderful *chinoiserie* wallpapers and beautiful furniture. Ferney, Voltaire's famous hide-out, which everyone doing the Grand Tour in his day visited (he received literally thousands of pilgrims), is also near. Lausanne, an hour away, is famous for its schools, university, and the Gothic Cathedral with its fine stained glass.

The mecca of all lovers of winter sports is SAINT MORITZ, in the Engadine, a sixty-mile-long valley in the southeast corner of the country. Saint Moritz was praised for its mineral springs by Paracelsus in 1539 and was known for them earlier still. Here are the Cresta and Suvretta runs; near here are Pontresina and Sils, and, best of all, Davos, with the Parsenn, the biggest open skiing area. The Küblis run, of seven miles, is the longest of all, and has been run in eleven minutes, while the average for a good skier *qui ne perd pas de temps* is half an hour. Other important ski centers are Klosters, Arosa, and Flims.

ZERMATT is to mountain climbing what Saint Moritz is to winter sports. From here the Gornergrat railway goes up the Riffelalp to Gornergrat, which is over 10,000 feet high. The view of Monte Rosa (15,217), the MATTERHORN (14,780), the Dent Blanche (14,318), the Weisshorn (14,804), and of many lesser peaks and glaciers is stupendous. All the mountains mentioned and many others can be climbed from Zermatt; and nearby is the RIFFELBERG RUN.

The Ticino, the Italian-speaking part of Switzerland south of the Saint Gotthard, has lovely lake resorts like Lugano, Locarno, and Ascona, a famous writers' and artists' colony. Poschiavo, beyond Pontresina, is the thriving center of the Poschiavo Valley, where vegetables and carnations are extensively grown. It has a late Gothic church and a Protestant one with archives containing the records of 140 witchcraft trials.

Everywhere in Switzerland—north, south, east, or west—the traveler always finds a perfect combination of sport, beauty, comfort, and hospitality.

ITALY

Open my heart, and you will see
Graved inside of it "Italy".
(De Gustibus)

As Greece was the source of western European culture, Rome was its unifier, its law giver, its mason, and road builder. The Roman Empire, once extending over the Mediterranean and over all western Europe, left behind it a common denominator in a language spoken from the days of the Republic till now. After Saint Peter's martyrdom at Rome, that city became the center from which Christianity spread to all corners of the earth.

Italy has so many children in her "boot" that the problem of the old woman who lived with hers in a shoe would hardly seem greater. This glistening "leg of Achilles" is 116,228 square miles with a population of some 46,598,000 people, loved the world over for their vitality and warmheartedness as much as for their country—for their speech, too, mellow as the flavor of Italian Chianti. Across the great avenues of Rome, the gondola-filled canals of Venice, the sunny piazzas of Florence pass some of the best-dressed women in the world. In the shops of the big cities are some of the best-designed modern textiles, furniture, and pottery to be found anywhere; while, over the dusty oxcart roads in the country, gnome-like modern automobiles dash from one museum town to the next.

Everywhere you go in northern Italy you look up in wonderment at the unequaled architecture of churches, cathedrals, palaces, and towers. Alongside the old there are often modern buildings, strangely harmonious, and the dwellings of the poor. Across cramped streets or courtyards where political discussions turn to arguments and the airing of purely personal grievances over dancing lines of wash, the settings vie with the picturesque patter—a window opened for a well-turned afterthought, shut, opened again for a final gesture with fist or garlic knife, and slammed again. Everything in demonstrative Italy turns to tears or laughter or song, frequently all three at once. For this is also the land of Leoncavallo and his Pagliacci, so beautifully sung at La Scala.

"Everything in Italy is not only cultivated but loved," writes the poet, Stephen Spender. "It is the country where the material is most often used to express human qualities. . . . It is as though in this country blood had veins which flowed through marble statues. This human expressiveness has affected the whole land, and it communicates itself everywhere." He writes today under the same enchantment that has fired all poets and all painters since the beginning of recorded time.

Italy has drawn all other nationals to it like a magnet; and the land Virgil and Goethe both sang is newly sung today by a young generation of poets and musicians in many languages, newly painted by many excellent contemporary artists, native and foreign.

Rome is seventeen hours by air from New York, three hours from London by the new jets; Naples is ten days by ship from the United States. Or if the traveler comes into Italy through the Brenner Pass, he first reaches Trentino, comprising the middle and upper valleys of the Adige which borders on Switzerland and Austria.

The Adamello-Presanella range, the over twelve-thousand-foot Ortler, the Brenta group and the DOLOMITES, with their extraordinary formations, including such giants as Marmolada and Cristallo, all rise suddenly from almost a sea-level plain. From Trent itself it is a bare eight miles to the summit of Monte Bordone, nearly five thousand feet; and from Lake Garda the road to Madonna di Campiglio, also over four thousand feet, seems to rise almost vertically.

TRENTINO is also a region of lovely FOLK COSTUMES, and countless lakes, from Lake Garda, thirty-five miles long and two to ten miles wide, to tiny mirrorlike pools scattered in the green of the woods or high in the eternal snows. Some, such as Caldonazzo and Levico, are well-known watering places; and Lavarone, Molveno, and Pergine Valsugana, are perfect too for swimming and water sports. There is a network of Alpine hostels in the mountains, and the trails are so well marked that climbers can spend weeks in the high hills without ever having to descend into the valleys.

On Lake Garda, Salò has a Gothic cathedral with frescoes by Palma the Younger. Riva, at the foot of the steep slopes of Monte Rochetta, is a delightful small town with excellent fishing. Trent, a bishopric since 1027, was the scene of the famous Oecumenical Council, which met from 1545 to 1563. The fountain of Neptune, the Piazza Cesare Battisti and the Romanesque Duomo, or Cathedral, are lovely, as is the grandiose Castello del Buon Consiglio, now a museum. Between Trent and Bolzano one of the roads crosses the Mendola pass at 4,462 feet, and offers a magnificent panorama of the Adige Valley, the Sarentini Mountains to the frontier, and the Brenta Dolomites. BOLZANO is a large industrial town, and also a first-class tourist center for climbing, skiing, or just plain scrambling. Merano, with its world-famous grape cure, and the most radioactive waters in Italy, is set at the foot of the Val Venosta and the Passeria valley. Cortina d'Ampezzo, with excellent ski slopes, a bobsled track, toboggan runs, ski jumps and skating rinks, is the site chosen for the 1956 winter Olympics.

Lake Como, one of the greatest of Italy's natural beauties, is thirty-five miles long and the deepest lake in Europe. It is on the Saint Gotthard route which links Italy with northern Europe. There are many lyrical towns on Como, "town after town with its russet-colored roofs, its church spire, its glimpse of some building or statue which seems the embodiment of genius": Cadenabbia, that inspired Longfellow; Menaggio; Varenna, with its mile-long gardens of rare flowers and trees; BELLAGIO, the Larian pearl, which is at the foot of the promontory that divides the lake in two. Bellagio has lovely old quarters, also excellent night clubs, tennis courts, and a gay social life.

Milan is the foremost industrial, commercial, and banking city of Italy. It lies in the heart of the Po plain, and faces the central massif of the Alps. The city has always been an international trade and exhibition center. MILAN CATHEDRAL is the largest and most complete Gothic building in Italy. Begun in 1387, it has 135 pinnacles, 2,245 statues, and wonderful fretwork in white marble. The Biblioteca Ambrosiana, with some half a million books and thirty thousand manuscripts, is one of the world's great libraries, and in the Dominican convent is the damaged "Last Supper" of Leonardo da Vinci. The city's opera season at La Scala is from December to May.

VERONA, the city of Romeo and Juliet and of "Two Gentlemen of Verona"; of Theodoric, who made it his capital; and of the Scaligers, is situated on the two banks of the Adige. Etruscan and Gallic before it became a Roman colony in 89 B.C., Verona has a splendid first-century Arena, with two series of mighty arcades. A lovely little twelfth-century church is situated beside the fine Roman theater where, since 1948, there has been a summer repertory of Shakespeare in Italian. Through the great arch next to the

Prefettura are the dwelling-place, church, and tombs of the Scaligers, the della Scala family, under whose rule Verona rosé to the height of its power in the thirteenth and fourteenth centuries. The Gothic tombs are splendid; and beyond, in the Piazza dei Signori, is the graceful Renaissance Loggia del Consiglio (erected 1476-1493, and restored in 1873). The Cathedral has an altarpiece by Titian, and the adjacent library is the oldest in Europe. San Zeno, a Romanesque basilica, built in the fifth century and later remodeled, gives an impression of "boundless space and height." Over the high altar is a Mantegna triptych of the Virgin and eight Saints. The red walls and fan-shaped battlements of the Castelvecchio, built in 1354 by Can Grande II, inspired the Kremlin's Red Square in Moscow. The PONTE SCALIGERO is one of six bridges crossing the Adige.

The earliest description of VENICE extant is by Cassiodorus, writing in the sixth century, when the inhabitants of the ancient cities of the Venetian plain fled to the little islands in the Lagoon. "Like the waterfowl," he writes, "they have spread their houses over the surface of the sea." Goethe, in the eighteenth century, tells how "little by little the dwellings rose, sand and marsh-land disappeared, giving place to solid stone, the houses fought for air like trees that are shut in, being forced to seek in height what was forbidden in breadth. Greedy for every inch of ground, . . . they left no more space than was sufficient to divide one row of houses from the other opposite, . . . for the rest the water served them for roads, piazzas and walks." It still does, in spite of the sidewalks and motorboats.

Venice is traversed by more than one hundred and fifty canals. The beautiful GRAND CANAL divides the city into two equal parts. The one Piazza is in front of the CATHEDRAL of SAINT MARK, and there are two Piazzettas, one outside the PALACE OF THE DOGES, and the other the Leoni. The city's transportation is provided by little steamers called *vaporetti;* by motorboats, canal barges, and ferries; and, of course, by GONDOLAS, the most graceful and colorful of boats, with their straw-hatted, red-sashed and opera-loving gondoliers. Every two years there is held in Venice an International Exhibition of Modern Art; and every year, in the late summer, Venice is the scene of the International Cinema Exhibition.

Marcel Proust compared the Venetian palaces to a "range of marble crags, at whose foot one goes in the evening by boat, to see the sunset." The Piazza of Saint Mark is like an immense outdoor drawing room, enclosed on three sides by arcades and on the fourth by the façade of the Cathedral, which was built in 830 to house the body of the saint. It is in Byzantine style, decorated with mosaics and marble, a façade in two tiers, a crown of ogee arches and Gothic tabernacles, and five Oriental domes. The Campanile, rebuilt 1902-1912, has Sansovino's lovely Loggetta (1540) next it, and on the north side of the square is the CLOCK TOWER, built in 1496, and telling not only the hour but the daily positions of moon and sun. On the west is the Old Library, Sansovino's masterpiece. The Palace of the Doges, whose fantastic Gothic exterior is lightened by an arcade with a loggia above it, and by large windows and balconies, is joined by the Bridge of Sighs to the prisons. Titian, Veronese and Tintoretto, Bellini, Tiepolo, and Sansovino decorated it. In the ACCADÉMIA DI BELLE ARTI is housed the most important collection of Venetian paintings, including Gentile Bellini's monumental "Recovery of the Relic of the Cross." Many of the best, however, are to be found in the churches. Santa Maria dei Miracoli, a jewel of the Venetian Renaissance, begun in 1481 by Pietro Lombardo, contains Pennacchi's Prophets and Saints, and Santi Giovanni e Paolo has a magnificent ceiling framing four paintings by Veronese. San Giovanni Crisostomo has a splendid Bellini, while San Sebastiano has no less than sixteen Veronese; and Santa Maria della Salute, Longhena's magnificent seventeenth-century church, has three Titians and a Tintoretto.

The Ca' d'Oro and the Ca' Rezzonico, where Browning died in 1889, are filled with collections of works of art set in the surroundings of patrician Venetian palaces. The latter reflects the time when Piazzetta and Tiepolo were the court painters of Europe, and Canaletto, Guardi and Longhi were the painters of the intimate life of Venice.

The Venetian feasts are great occasions: for example, there is the Feast of Saint Mark, in April, when young men give rosebuds to their sweethearts; the Regatta on the Grand Canal with its procession of gilded barges; and the Feast of the Redeemer on the third Sunday in July, with illuminated barges and fireworks.

The Lido is no longer the wild and lonely heath where Schopenhauer brooded and Byron rode, but one of the most famous and fashionable sea resorts in Europe. Everyone dances and swims—there are municipal cabañas for very little, and cabañas on the beaches of great hotels for very much. There is a casino, too, for a change of pace and money. At Torcello, there is a wonderful ninth-century church and a lovely cathedral founded in 639, while at Murano is the home of the blown-glass industry that has made Venetian glass famous the world over.

The Italian Riviera is full of delightful resorts, combining the pleasures of water and mountains, for always behind the towns stand the waiting Alps. Viareggio, near Lucca, once a tiny port, is now primarily an elegant modern year-round bathing resort. PORTOFINO, near Genoa and a short drive from fashionable Rapallo, is one of the most attractive small ports anywhere. The houses, color-washed in various hues, are set in a gay horseshoe pattern along the water's edge. The little harbor is full of fishing boats, and on the peninsula are a charming castle and several villas. The hotels are excellent and the climate perfect. Here Saint George's body was left by Saint Louis—and ironically, was bombed by the British in World War II! Through a two-mile tunnel one may travel to CAMOGLI, another attractive old seaport almost as idyllic as Portofino.

Lucca, surrounded by its sixteenth-century ramparts, has many churches, including the lovely SAINT MICHAEL'S with its light and airy façade, and the Cathedral of Saint Martin, begun in 1060, and built of black and white marble. Within the Cathedral is the touching tomb of Ilaria del Carretto and a crucifix carved, according to legend, by Nicodemus and miraculously brought to Lucca in 782. Charles Morgan, entranced with Lucca, centered his novel, *Sparkenbroke,* in and around the city.

Pisa, seven miles from the sea on the Arno, where Galileo was born, is world-famous for its LEANING TOWER, one of four astonishing buildings grouped together. The others are the Cathedral, the Baptistery and the Campo Santo. The marble Campanile, which is the Leaning Tower, was begun in 1174 and completed around 1350. It slipped with the land, but is still intact. Leaning more than sixteen feet out of perpendicular, 294 steps lead dizzily to the top.

Of all the Tuscan towns, in that landscape where "the hills have a pale-green, almost bluish color and quality as though the sky were melting into landscape and the landscape into the sky," SAN GIMIGNANO, on a hill about forty miles from Florence, provides the closest evocation of a medieval Italian town. There were seventy-six towers, of which eleven survive. The steep, narrow streets and splendid palaces, with their elegant windows; the Romanesque Duomo; the Ghirlandajo frescoes, and the 1288 Town Hall form a spectacular unity.

FLORENCE has both produced and attracted to her more great men than any other city in the world that is not a nation's capital. And she is one of the most beautiful—if not *the* most beautiful of all cities. Dante was born and spent his youth in Florence; Petrarch and Boccaccio became close friends there. Milton, Montaigne, Heine, the Brownings, D'Annunzio, Mark Twain, Rilke, these are but a few of those who came to her and stayed. Milton's

> I sing, and my good people hear me not;
> Though dear the Thames, no less is Arno dear

contrasts with Macaulay's Jacobite who

> Mourned by Arno for my lovelier Tees

but both loved Florence and her treasures. The Piazza del Duomo forms the center of the town. Here is Brunelleschi's Dome, which in 1436 completed the Gothic CATHEDRAL OF SANTA MARIA DEL FIORE, faced with white, green, and red marble. Giotto's Campanile, begun in 1334, is richly covered with bas-reliefs by Andrea Pisano and Luca della Robbia; three stories of splendid windows and a cornice crown the whole. The Baptistery is chiefly famous for the three great bronze doors—one by Andrea Pisano, two by Ghiberti. Or San Michele, built between 1337 and 1404, is an oratory with Donatello statues, and a tabernacle.

The majestic Palazzo Vecchio, on the PIAZZA DELLA SIGNORIA, was once the home of Cosimo de' Medici. The great Sala dei Cinquecento, built in 1495, on Savonarola's advice, housed the Council of the Republic that was created on the expulsion of the Medici. On the steps are the heraldic lion of Florence, Donatello's "Judith and Holofernes," and a copy of the Michelangelo "David." The Palazzo Riccardi is another of the famous Medici houses. The Uffizi contains the richest collection of paintings in the world, including the "Primavera" and the BIRTH OF VENUS of Botticelli, painted for Lorenzo de' Medici, the "Pope Julius II" of Raphael, and Michelangelo's "Holy Family." Additions to the original Medici collections have been made to the present time. The PONTE VECCHIO, the city's oldest bridge, rebuilt in 1345 and spared by the Germans, is lined with jewelers', goldsmiths', and silversmiths' shops. It is a good spot from which to watch the fireworks on Saint John's Day in midsummer.

The Pitti Palace for many years the residence of the rulers of the city is beautifully furnished, and it houses pictures by Raphael, Andrea del Sarto, Titian, and Rubens and very many more. Surrounding the Pitti are the delicious Boboli Gardens, where open-air theater and excellent concerts take place. The Church of Santo Spirito has several paintings by Filippino Lippi. In addition, every traveler should see the Church of Santa Maria Novella; the Medicean Chapels with the New Sacristy by Michelangelo; the Fra Angelico frescoes at San Marco; the Donatellos in the sacristy of San Lorenzo; the Gozzolis in the Palazzo Riccardi; Santa Croce with the Giotto frescoes and the tombs of Michelangelo and Machiavelli;

and San Miniato al Monte, crowning the Viale dei Colli.

Each province of Italy has its deeply differentiated people. Along the Tuscan road, where the "Juno-eyed" white oxen pull oxCARTS no different from those the Etruscans used, the language will be richer, more mellifluous than in the Umbrian uplands, where Saint Francis walked with his earth-brown followers. In the south, the mountainy men of the Basilicata are serious and dignified, while the Neapolitans are the quickest, most lizard-like of people. And the Romans still bear in their grave, noble faces, the memory of "Roma nobilis, urbs et Domina" —noble Rome, city and queen.

SIENA sits high on three hills overlooking the Arbia Valley, wholly walled, a town of brick palaces and winding streets. The thirteenth-century CATHEDRAL, with its triple-sabled façade by Giovanni Pisano, was for Richard Wagner "a marble realization of the temple of the Graal." It has sculptures by Bernini and Donatello's exquisite Saint John, Pinturicchio frescoes, and an octagonal marble pulpit by Nicola Pisano. The pavement is unique, forming a series of polychromic marble engravings.

The PALAZZO PUBBLICO with its graceful Mangia tower, overlooking the Campo square and the Loggia; the many fountains; and the six hundred Sienese paintings in the Pinacoteca are all wonderful. The Palio della Contrade, the great summer horse race in the Campo square, is held once in July and again in August, and is Siena's chief event; the townsfolk wear their ancient liveries, the big bells toll and everyone goes wild with excitement.

At AREZZO, too, the birthplace of Petrarch and Vasari, there are thrills and pageantry twice a year at the Joust of the Saracen, a traditional medieval tournament held in June and September, commemorating the battles against the Saracens during the Crusades.

Perugia, an Etruscan town overlooking the Tiber, has lovely medieval buildings and many pictures of the Umbrian School of painting; the streets are named as they might be in Paradise, for saints and angels and the Trinity Itself. The Collegio del Cambio with the Perugino frescoes; the crenellated Palazzo Comunale; the great fountain with reliefs by Nicola and Giovanni Pisano; the oratory of San Bernardino; the churches of San Domenico (1305); San Pietro (tenth century); and, above all, the tomb of the Volumni, the finest remaining Etruscan sculpture, are all sights not easily forgotten.

ASSISI is the most single-minded town in the world. Near the station, is the Church of Santa Maria degli Angeli. Here, under the dome, is the Porziuncola Chapel, which Saint Francis repaired with his own hands, and the cell in which he died. Up in the town is the Double Church of SAINT FRANCIS. On the lower nave walls of the UPPER CHURCH are the great frescoes of the saint's life by Giotto and his pupils. Cimabue, Simone Martini, and Lorenzetti also decorated the light, airy hall in pure Gothic.

Around Assisi's convent gate
The birds, God's poor who cannot wait,
From moor and mere and darksome wood
Came flocking for their dole of food.
(Longfellow)

Saint Clare's body lies in the crypt of Santa Chiara and in the Chapel of the Sacrament is the Crucifix which is reputed to have spoken to Saint Francis. From Assisi one can walk up to San Damiano, where Saint Francis received Saint Clare; and uphill all the way for three miles is the Carceri, a monastery in the heart of an ilex-tree forest where Saint Francis loved to retire to pray. His bed, dug in the rock, is still there; and here, in spring, the scillas and grape hyacinths and hepaticas grow profusely to the snow's edge.

Urbino, Raphael's birthplace, with the National Gallery of the Marches; Foligno, with memories of Saint Angela and admirable pictures; Spoleto, on a hill crowned by the Rocca; and Orvieto, on an isolated, rocky plateau, are unique and crowded with treasures. The Orvieto CATHEDRAL, started in 1290, is magnificently built and richly ornamented; the five columns and the Fra Angelico and Signorelli frescoes in the chapel of San Brizio are fabulous.

And so, since all roads lead there, at last: "*Ecco Roma*" as the postillions cried when first the city appeared before them. Today, as Eleanor Clark writes in *Rome and a Villa,* the traveler sees: ". . . a city of bells and hills and walls . . . of many trees, nordic and tropical together, pine, ilex and palm, and water and a disturbing depth of shadows, of acres of ruins, some handsome, some shabby lumps and dumps of useless masonry, sprinkled through acres of howling modernity . . ."

ROME can best be seen, said Pope Pius IX, in three days, or three years. And in three days the best thing is first to drive up and down all the seven hills and see the outsides of the COLOSSEUM; the ROMAN FORUM; the Palazzo Venezia; the three basilicas [Saint John Lateran, Santa Maria Maggiore, and San Paolo fuori le mura]; the Campidoglio, designed by Michelangelo, with the great statue of Marcus Aurelius; the Quirinal; the Scala Santa; the Pantheon; the Circus Maximus; the Baths of Caracalla (where the most splendid operas are given nightly through the summer); the Roman Capitol; the Spanish Steps; the graves of Shelley and Keats; the Piazza di Spagna; the arches of Constantine, Titus, Septimius Severus, and five others; the Basilica Iulia; the Baths of Diocletian; the first-rate new railway station; the Corso, with the Piazza Colonna and the Column of Marcus Aurelius; the Piazza del Populo; the Pincio, with the gardens wherein is the Villa Borghese; the Villa Medici; the Mausoleum of Augustus and the Ara Pacis; Il Gesù; the PIAZZA NAVONA with its FOUNTAINS; the great bridge of Saint Angelo, built by Hadrian; and the sinister Castle of Saint Angelo; the Pyramid of Cestius; and, of course, Saint Peter's and the Vatican, guarded by the SWISS GUARDS.

Then go inside—anywhere—and your three days will be three years before you are done. The Catacombs, a drive along the Appian Way, the Sistine Chapel, and the Venus Anadyomene; the Villa d'Este, and the Villa of Hadrian in nearby Tivoli are among the many essentials to everyone's Roman holiday.

From Naples, spread fanwise above one of the loveliest bays in the world and looking across to VESUVIUS, POMPEII and Herculaneum, buried by the eruption in the year 79, can be visited. Here are entire towns, much as their inhabitants left them, nearly 1900 years ago. Theaters, temples, private houses, frescoes, mosaics, statues, domestic utensils, all are to be seen; plates, cups, make-up, bathrooms, the dry cleaners and the grocery store, the hospital and the vegetable market; nothing of this rich provincial town seems to be hidden from us.

Down the coast from Naples are Ischia and the delightful Isle of CAPRI with its Blue Grotto; still lower down the "heel" is lovely POSITANO, a small white town built at equal distance from Sorrento and Amalfi. The oriental-looking houses, with their round-topped roofs, are sharply outlined against the dark green citrus fruit trees; they cling fast to the steep slope that runs sheer into the sea, foaming with orange blossoms. AMALFI has a lovely emerald grotto and a Cathedral with a magnificent majolica-adorned steeple; it also has one of the most heavenly coastal drives in Italy. Paestum has the Greek Doric Temples, golden and perfect after more than two thousand years.

From Naples there are boats to Palermo, the capital of Sicily, and of Norman, Greek, and Arab art. Here are the Cappella Palatina, a jewel of Arab-Norman architecture and mosaics; the Cathedral with the tomb of Frederick II; the Palazzo Reale, and above all Monreale, built by William II in 1174, and housing the most complete series of mosaics anywhere.

Sicily is a whole world—and several civilizations—in itself: the Greek theater at TAORMINA; the Ear of Dionysius—the grim rock prison—at Syracuse, and the theater and quarry there; the temples at Agrigento, and the most perfect single Greek temple in the world at Segesta; the high town of Enna where, by Lake Pergusa, as Milton wrote:

> . . . Proserpine gathering flowers,
> Herself a fairer flower, by gloomy Dis
> Was gathered . . .

all are places of cultural as well as spiritual and historical pilgrimage.

GERMANY

Hamburg, one of the world's greatest ports. General view of the city, with the City Hall and square in foreground.

Hanover. The City Hall was completed shortly before World War I.

Hans Hartz

Eduard Renner

Molzahn-Althe.

Market Square and old Church of Saint Aegidius in Osterode, Lower Saxony, health resort in the Harz Mountains.

View from the town hall in Goslar, Brunswick. The town first became well known under Otto the Great with the discovery of local minerals.

Wolf Strache

Welbergen Castle, near Ochtrup, Westphalia, reflects the past in a natural water setting.

Fishing boats at Lorelei Rock on the Rhine. Its echo gave rise to the legend of the Lorelei siren. The Nibelung treasure was hidden here.

Picturesque houses at Monschau in the Eifel area of the Rhineland.

Frankfurt on Main, capital of Hesse, birthplace of Goethe, and a leading commercial, literary, and art center. The **Römer** has been restored since World War II.

Vierzehnheiligen, pilgrim church in Franconia, Bavaria, reconstructed (1745–1772) under Balthasar Neumann, is a superb example of German baroque.

Rehns, thirteenth-century walled town of the Middle Rhine, near Koblenz.

Eduard Renner

Eduard Renner

Griffin sign in Dinkelsbühl, Fraconia, along the romantic rothrough Bavaria to Würzburg.

Nördlingen, Franconia, anothbeautifully preserved old Bavian town. It witnessed two battof the Thirty Years' War, in 16
and 1645.

he quaint 1724 Town Hall at
irchheim, in Württemberg-
aden, on the Teck River.

odtmoos, Württemberg-Baden,
typical Black Forest village,
d spa.

Eduard Renner

arl Seufert

151

Kostich

Outside Garmisch-Partenkirchen, ⊂
the road from Munich to Salzburg.

Kirche in der Wies (Church-in-the
Meadow), the lightest and one of th
most glorious of the Bavarian baroqu
churches.

Luis Demmeler

Kostich

Neuschwanstein Castle, near Füssen, Bavaria, one of the castles of fantasy- and Wagner-loving King Ludwig II.

Linderhof Castle, in the B
varian mountains, anoth
of Ludwig II's dream castl
near Oberammergau.

Ewing Krainin

Bavarian mountaineers
the town square of Berchte
gaden. Near here was H
ler's mountain retreat.

Burton Holmes

Kostich

...berammergau, well-known ...r its painted houses and ...lk costumes, and for the ...ssion Play given every ten ...ars.

...leersburg, South Baden, on ...ake Constance. Germany ...ares the lake with Austria ...d Switzerland.

Ewing Galloway

Benes

Vodnyansky

A U S T R I A

Above: Beethoven's House outside Vienna, where the composer wrote the "Eroica" symphony. *Right:* Heiligenkreuz, baroque corner of the monastery courtyard, near Vienna.

Vodnyansky

posite: Vienna. Belvedere (1717–1724), the palace of Prince Eugene of Savoy.

Kosti Ruohomaa

students at Salzburg, with Untersberg mountain in the background.

Karnitschnigg

Opposite: Salzburg, looking toward Hohensa
burg fortress. *Opposite, bottom:* Innsbruck, ca
ital of the Tirol and center of ski traffic.

Above: Street sign in Salzburg (1639). *Right:*
Salzburg at night during the festival season.

Sabine We

Kostich

Characteristic landscape in the beautiful Inn vall‹

oss

WITZERLAND

bove: Saint Gallen, named after St. all, Irish missionary who lived here m 614–640.

ight: The old fortified town of Schaff-ausen, on the Rhine. The fifteenth-ntury bell of Schiller's "Song of the ell" and Longfellow's "Golden Leg-d" is near the minster.

W. Suschitzky

161

Tod Webb (E.

Brunnen, on Lake Lucerne, a favorite stop with tourists.

Interior of a house in Zurich, prosperous industrial and intellectual capital of German-speaking Switzerland.

E. A. Heiniger

Kostich

Near Interlaken, Bern canton, gateway to the glittering snow- and glacier-covered Bernese Alps.

E. Gyger

The Eiger, Mönch, and Jungfrau, in the Bernese Alps, near Mürren.

Wide World

Fransioli

Above: Springtime in Montreux, French-speaking city on the Lake of Geneva.

Geneva. Rue Calvin, in the old city, named after the sixteenth-century reformer whose work was done here.

Opposite: Night view of Bern, the historic, lovely federal capital of Switzerland. In foreground is the bear pit maintained since 1513.

E. Gyger

Toni Frissell

Snow-capped trees on the slopes of Adelboden, canton of Bern.

Time out at a ski hut on the Riffelberg run near Zermatt.

Opposite: Above Zermatt, Valais, the skiing and climbing center.

166

Toni Frissell

The Matterhorn, 14,780-foot mountain peak near Zermatt, reflected in Riffelsee. *Below:* Saint-Moritz, Graubünden. View over Lakes Silvaplana and Sils.

ITALY

Summer in the Dolomites.

I.S

Dolomites near Bolzano, Tre
tino, south of the Brenner Pas

Traditional folk costume in th
Dolomites.

Kostich

...yside shrine in Trentino.

...r street in picturesque Bel-
...o on Lake Como, Lombardy.

I.S.T.

View from Milan Cathedral in the prosperous industrial capital of Lombardy.
Below: Ponte Scaligero in Verona, colorful setting of "Romeo and Juliet."

Venice. Bronze equestrian statue on Saint Mark's. Behind is the clock tower.

Fritz Henle

Ewing Krainin

Venice. The Grand Canal. *Below:* The Piazzetta and Palace of the Doges. Saint Mark's and clock tower are in backgro

Ivan Dmitri

(American Export Lin

sitors at the Academy study Gentile Bellini's "Recovery of the Relic of the Cross" as if viewing medieval Venice rough a window.

Cresta

Camogli, Liguria, a lovely old town on the Italian Riviera

n Gimignano, Tuscany, noted for its medieval towers and frescoes.

Fritz Henle

Ivan Dmitri

The fishing village of Portofino, a short drive from Rapallo, on the Riviera.

Kostich

Tuscany. *Above:* The Leaning Tower of Pisa. *Opposite, top:* The Church of Saint Michael, Lucca, with its light and airy façade and Romanesque campanile. *Opposite:* Oxcarts on a village street near Florence.

Florence. *Right:* Piazza della Signoria from Loggia dei Lanzi, with its famous sculptures. *Below:* "Birth of Venus" by Botticelli, in the Uffizi. *Opposite:* Side view of the Cathedral of Santa Maria del Fiore, begun in 1296, faced with white, green, and red marble.

Three Lio.

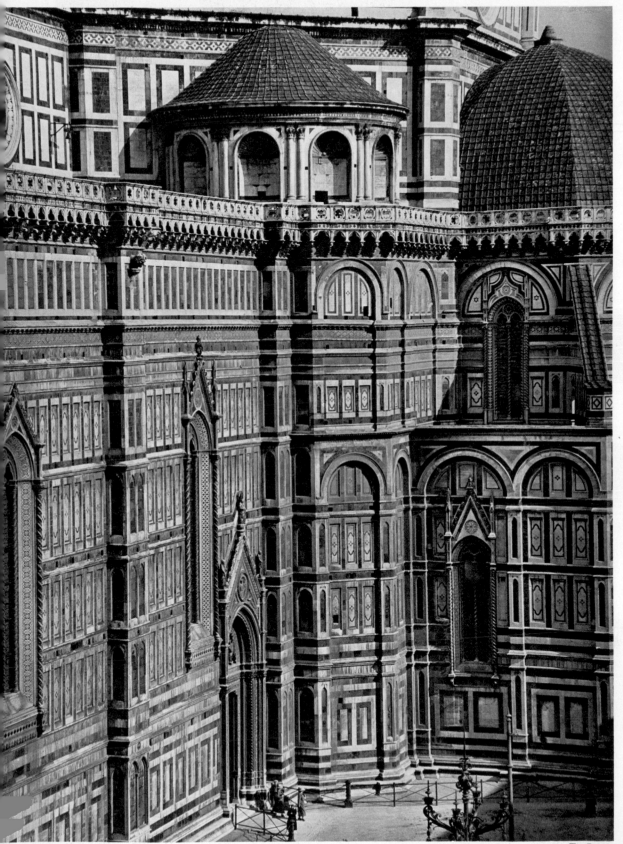

Tet Borsig

Ewing Krain

Florence. The Ponte Vecchio, oldest bridge in the city, was rebuilt in 1345.

Medieval pageantry is revived twice a year at the tournament in Arezzo, the native town of Petrarch and Vasari.

Opposite: Siena. View over the Palazzo Pubblico, the finest Gothic palace in Tuscany, to the Cathedral, described by Wagner as "a marble realization of the temple of the Graal."

I.S.T.

Tet Borsig

Assisi, Umbria, owes its fame to Saint Francis who was born and who died here. The Upper Church of Saint Francis. *Left:* One of the Giotto frescoes.

Opposite: Orvieto, Umbria. Façade of the marble Cathedral, landmark of the Etruscan town which in the old days was repeatedly at war with Siena.

Martin Hürlimann

Ewing Krain

Evans

Rome. The Colosseum, begun b
Vespasian and completed b
Titus A.D. 80.

Fountain of Neptune, one o
three great fountains in Rome
Piazza Navona.

Opposite: Swiss Guards at th
Vatican dressed as they hav
been since the sixteenth century

Herbert List

"I came, I saw, I conquered." The statue of Julius Caesar on the Roman Forum.

Rome, seen from the top of Saint Peter's. *Below:* Pompeii, and Vesuvius which ruined the city A.D. 79.

Kostich

Amalfi, Campania, oldest Italian maritime republic. The Amalfi drive is one of the
most spectacular scenic routes in Italy.

Fritz Henle

[c]olorful boats along the beach at Positano, Campania, harbor town lying halfway
[b]etween Sorrento and Amalfi.

191

Capri, island resort since Roman times. *Below:* The Greek theater at Taormina, Sicily.

GREECE

"All European architecture, bad and good, old and new, is derived from Greece through Rome, and colored and perfected from the east." So wrote John Ruskin; but it is not only architecture that we derive from Greece. The pursuit of beauty and truth, in so far as we apprehend them, is part of our heritage from the "glory that was Greece"; as our law stems from the "grandeur that was Rome," and our religion from the Jews; "we are all spiritual Semites."

Greece is a kingdom in the southern part of the Balkan Peninsula. The mainland is 41,328 square miles and the total area is 51,843, including the islands. The vast majority of Greeks, who now total nearly eight million, are Greek Orthodox by religion, and most of them earn their livelihood from the land. Wine, olives, tangerines, currants, figs, and tobacco are the important harvests.

Less than fifty miles from Athens, the capital, is Cape Colonna (Sunium). On top of a high rocky promontory are the weathered marble columns of the Doric Temple of Poseidon, God of the Sea. Built in the fifth century B.C. to watch over and protect the ancient seamen homeward bound to Athens, the temple originally had six columns at each end and thirteen on each side. Byron carved his name on one of the few that are left, and elsewhere wrote:

Place me on Sunium's marble steep,
Where nothing save the waves and I
May hear our mutual murmurs sweep.

ATHENS has a temperate climate; indeed the ancients claimed that the sunny plains and bracing air of Attica fostered the intellectual and aesthetic nature of the Athenians. Seen from the air, its thousands of stucco houses, its dug-out hillsides, and its rounded mountain tops have a creamy, yellowish look, though from Athens itself one can see the wooded slopes of the neighboring mountains. The highest promontory in the Athenian landscape is MOUNT LYCABETTUS (Hagios Georgios), with the Chapel of Saint George at the summit; and the most famous building in the world is the Parthenon on the ACROPOLIS, the rocky oblong tableland fortified around 2000 B.C.

THE PARTHENON ("chamber of the Virgin") and the other Acropolis monuments are approached through Mnesicles' partially finished but most impressive gateway, the Propylaea. Built in the fifth century B.C. by Ictinus and Callicrates under Pericles, and chiefly ornamented by Phidias, whom Plato called "a wise stone-cutter," the Parthenon "has not a straight line in it." All the Doric columns lean inward, and the shafts have convex silhouettes. Respected by the Romans, the building, along with the other temples, was converted into a church in the sixth century after Christ (Phidias' statue of Athena was plundered during an invasion by Barbars) and after 1466 into a mosque, complete with minaret.

On the Acropolis are three temples: the Parthenon itself, "the best gem upon her zone"; the Erechtheum and the temple of Athena Nike. The ERECHTHEUM is Ionian to the Parthenon's Doric, and elegant and feminine in contrast to the Parthenon's grave masculinity. It still has five of the nine original caryatids; a sixth is in London's British Museum. It is said that the young Grecian girls used as models came from Caryae, in Laconia. The Erechtheum was named after Erechtheus, the legendary founder of Athens, and was dedicated to Athena Polias, protectress of the city.

The graceful TEMPLE OF ATHENA NIKE, begun after 450 B.C., destroyed by the Turks in 1687, and reconstructed from remnants in 1835, consists of a cella 12 feet by 9, with an Ionic porch of four fluted columns. The bas-reliefs of the frieze were replaced on the east and south sides; those of the north and west were looted by Lord Elgin, and, together with the great frieze from the Parthenon, are housed in the British Museum.

Traces of the Hecatompedon, an archaic temple built about the time of Solon (sixth century B.C.) are also to be found on the Acropolis. And the small museum built among the rocks contains the statue of Hercules wrestling with a Triton in the presence of a wonderfully pleasant and attractive monster with three human heads, all with the kindliest expression; the Moscophorus, or calf-carrier; and Nike tying her sandal. Also on or around the slopes of the Acropolis are: the Theater of Dionysus, where Greek drama reached its highest expression with performances of Sophocles, Euripides, Aristophanes and others; the Asclepieum, or temple of Asclepius, the god of medicine; the Odeum of Herodes Atticus (after A.D. 161); and the Porch of Eumenes, built in 197 B.C.

The Areopagus, a hill consecrated to Ares, the God of War, and to the Eumenides, or Furies, was the seat of the supreme court of the Athenian republic, and also a sanctuary where murderers and other shady characters took refuge. Here, it is said, Orestes came after killing his adulterous, murderess mother, Clytemnestra; here Demosthenes was condemned in 324 B.C.; here Phryne, the courtesan, was pardoned, because she was so beautiful. Here too A.D. 60 came Saint Paul, who spoke of the Unknown God and converted Dionysius the Areopagite.

Today, as in Pindar's day, "the heart of Athens, streaming with oblations, is widethronged with many a face," and modern Athens, clean, busy and gay with its more than half a million inhabitants, is centered upon Omonia Square, where many of the best cafés do a thriving business. The gardens of the Zappeion are most attractive, especially when the trees are illuminated at night. Constitution Square, with the white marble facade of the palace, and the busy Stadion and University streets are always crowded. Yannakis, the most famous café in Athens, is the center for news, gossip, and political canards: the Greeks are still, as they were in Aristotle's day, most politically minded, and they regard anyone uninterested in current affairs as indeed a beast (or a god). Ouzo, the cloudy Greek Pernod, and *retsina,* the light resinated wine that tastes, to the uninitiated, of turpentine, are, with Turkish coffee in tiny cups, the commonest drinks. Their water, highly regarded by both the Greeks and their guests, is also much drunk, especially with the delicious sticky desserts, pastries or exotic confitures.

The "Tower of the Winds," near the Gate of Athena Archegetis, is really the clock tower of Andronicus. Built in the first century B.C., it is octagonal, with an allegorical frieze representing the eight winds. On top was a bronze Triton that pointed the direction of the wind. The TEMPLE OF ZEUS "wherein the Greek deity found in Athens the Heaven he left behind" was started by King Antiochus and completed by Hadrian. Vitruvius said that the temple was "the only one in the world conceived on a scale proportionate to the majesty of the God." On the first Monday in Lent, popular dances take place there.

The EVZONES, soldiers in national costume, who guard the king's Palace and the Tomb of the Unknown Soldier (in front of the Parliament Building), are all dressed up in white pleated skirts, white baggy-sleeved blouses, boleros, soft shoes with enormous pompons, and tiny red caps. The changing of the guard is as popular a sight in Athens as it is in London or Copenhagen.

It is only seven miles from Athens to Daphne where stands the lovely eleventh-century Byzantine Convent of the Dormition of the Virgin, with its splendid mosaics. And from Athens it is only fifteen miles to Eleusis, today called Lefsina. One can travel there by car or train, and take in the splendid view of the bay. Eleusis is a poor village of some three thousand inhabitants, almost all of Albanian descent; it has a soap factory and a cement works, as well as a distillery. Here, in the days of the ancients, was the center of the worship of the great goddesses, Demeter and her beautiful daughter Persephone, whom Pluto carried off to the underworld, and whom her mother recovered annually for six months in the year. The feasts of the goddesses were in February and September, when Greeks came from Athens and all over Greece to celebrate the Mysteries and become initiates. The ruins of the sanctuary were surrounded by a great wall, for none but the initiates might enter. Aeschylus was born at Eleusis in 525 B.C.

Thebes, ancient rival of Athens, where Oedipus unknowingly slew his father, solved the riddle of the Sphinx, was proclaimed king, and discovered himself husband of his own mother, is still lively, though a modern town, entirely rebuilt since the earthquake of 1893. And Levádeia, the old Turkish capital of Boeotia, is on the slopes of the gorge of Hercyna, with Mount Elikon above it, crowned with a Frankish castle. Levádeia has white houses with balconies over the stream, bridges, windmills, a bazaar, good churches and mosques, and a splendid view of Helicon and Parnassus, once dedicated to Bacchus and to Apollo and the Muses.

Návpaktos is on the harbor where the Turkish fleet put in after the battle of Lepanto, when Don John of Austria and Prince Andrea Doria beat 250 Turkish galleys, and Cervantes lost the use of an arm, on October 7, 1571.

DELPHI, the most beautiful site in Greece, has "mystery, grandeur, and a holy awe." Naturally shaped like a theater, as Strabo remarked, "in the center of a colossal enclosure of bare rocks, the temple splendidly dominates the tragic solitude." The Phaedriades (Shining) rocks, from which the sacrilegious were thrown, are still dazzling. The ground is prone to earthquakes, and terrible storms thundering down from Parnassus have scarred and moved the rocks. The vapors that escape from the fissures in the chalk and the springs that gush out were both considered sacred. The sanctuary was consecrated to Apollo, whose Pythian priestess would sit on the sacred tripod, uttering the ambiguous words of the oracle in verse.

On the MARMARIA at Delphi is the tholos, a marble rotunda with Corinthian columns, and the Doric temples of Athena Pronaia and Athena Ergane. The gymnasium, the baths, the fountain of Kastalia are also at the same level. Above is the hieron of Apollo, with many terraces, linked by a sacred way, with votive statues on either side. Within a rough circle of rocks, and close to a great fissure from which vapors rise, is the Sibyl's rock, on the site of the primitive oracle of Ge-Themis (the great mother) which was guarded by the serpent Python which Apollo slew "with an immortal's vengeance." The remains of the temple of Apollo (built in 329 B.C.) are on the site of several far earlier structures. Of the ancient town the theater, the stadium, and many tombs still remain. Over a thousand feet below is the sea, the Gulf of Corinth, beyond which lies the land of Creusa, Princess of Corinth, for whom Jason deserted the fanatical Medea. The Delphi museum contains many treasures, including friezes from the temples, a colossal Sphinx, statues, and the dancers from the Acanthus Column. From the top of nearby Parnassus (over seven thousand feet) the dawn shows Mount Athos, Pelion, Ossa, MOUNT OLYMPUS (the seat of the gods), Helicon and even, it was said, Constantinople!

Olympia is set in a landscape absolutely contrary to that around Delphi. Idyllic and serene, in a green valley through which the Alpheus flows, verdant slopes and wooded glades envelope the ruins with quiet and peace. Set at the foot of Mount Cronion, Olympia was never a city but a vast sanctuary of Zeus. Here was proclaimed a sacred truce, which enabled the Greeks, torn by civil wars and internecine fights, to meet and worship there in safety and to achieve a momentary sense of unity. Here the Olympic games were held. Olympia was a place of active worship for over a thousand years, from archaic times until the reign of Theodosius II (A.D. 408-450), when the temple of Zeus was destroyed.

The best view of Olympia is from the slopes of Mount Cronion, though it is hard to see the ruins in their totality, owing to the trees. The temple of Hera (Heraeum), one of the oldest Doric temples known, contained the holy vessels of the Altis. Near the Pelopium and the great altar of Zeus, on a high terrace, are the ruins of the greatest and richest temple of all Greece, that of Zeus. The twelve Treasure Houses, erected by the Greek states, were small chapels for offerings, and the Leonidaeum, an immense rectangle, was probably a hotel for distinguished guests. The sites of Phidias' studio and of the priestly college and numerous other buildings are shown. In the Museum are magnificent sculptures, including the Hermes of Praxiteles, and equally famous APOLLO and the Centaurs (from the west gable of the temple). With outstretched arm, Apollo rebukes the centaurs:

> Out of my shrine I charge you. Hence! begone!
> Avoid this holy ground. Go instantly!
> . . . Oh loathsome, heaven-detested creatures . . .
>
> (Translated by J. T. Sheppard)

Aeschylus thus wrote of Apollo and the Furies in *Eumenides,* his drama of the manners and morals of the gods.

In the *Iliad,* Poseidon is described on the summit of Samothrace surveying the plain of Troy. More talked about was the discovery there in 1863 of the "Victory of Samothrace," which went to France. People still return to Nike's home town for its hot sulphur springs. Across the blue Aegean, to the north, is western THRACE with its mixed population who grow tobacco, make cheeses, and tend sheep in this hilly and cloudy "land of the Boreas."

To the west is Salonika, second in size to Athens, and from here the Chalcidice peninsula is within easy reach, down to MOUNT ATHOS. This small monastic republic is some forty miles long, and consists of a ridge of limestone rising from fifteen hundred feet to an isolated peak six thousand feet high, of white marble, which is Mount Athos proper. The first monastery was supposedly founded by Constantine the Great, although there is no material evidence of any foundation before that of the Great Lavra in 963.

At one time there were over fifty orthodox monasteries; now there are twenty, including the famous SAINT DENIS. The architecture varies in style, from the end of the tenth to the end of the fourteenth centuries. There are numberless frescoes, and of the nine thousand manuscripts, about a fourth are beautifully illuminated. The monasteries of the Holy Mountain have always been hospitable, and male travelers may stay there freely. No women are allowed, nor even cows or hens! The monks have fallen on evil days financially, and, owing to the cessation of contributions from countries east of the Iron Curtain and from Russia itself, are extremely poor. The other great Greek mon-

asteries are the Meteora, in Thessaly. Situated high up on rocky crags, they can be reached only by rope ladders or in a net wound up by windlasses.

On the Peloponnesian peninsula, the convent of the Megaspileon, or Great Grotto (women are allowed to visit here), is perched on a naked rock three hundred feet high. It has a church with admirable mosaics and a library of several hundred manuscripts. It is near Kalavryta, a green and peaceful village where on Sunday, December 12, 1943, the Germans shot 1400 men to death and would have burned the women and children but the Austrian guard, losing his nerve, allowed them to escape.

Mistra, just outside of Sparta, is a complete Byzantine town. Monemvasia (which gave its name to Malmsey wine) and Modon, a Mycenaean town also on a promontory, both have splendid Venetian remains.

Rhodes, the largest of the Dodecanese Islands, was once the site of the Colossus, the ancient world's sixth wonder. The Crusaders' castle of the Grand Master of the Knights of Saint John is well preserved and the island is filled with Turkish monuments, buildings, cemeteries, and medieval buildings of the chevaliers who ruled from 1309 to 1522. Nearly three hundred miles east lies Cyprus, British owned, and populated largely by Greeks, and by Turks and other nationalities. Cyprus is famous, among other things, for the legendary waters that gave birth to Venus, the town where crusading Richard Coeur de Lion was married, and the still-standing castle of Othello at Famagusta.

Largest of the Greek-owned islands is olive-growing Crete, where Jupiter, disguised as a bull, surprised Europa. Here also the great Minoan palace was unearthed at Knossos and here, from Candia, El Greco sailed to Venice on his way to Spain.

The smallest of the Cyclades, and one of the most interesting, archaelogically, is Delos, with its marble-paved quay. The island gave birth to Apollo and Artemis, and here "burning Sappho loved and sung." The ruins today give a picture of archaic Greek life and can be compared with Roman Pompeii. The Sacred Lake, now empty, is guarded by STONE LIONS; many of the mosaics remain on the floors of the houses, including Cleopatra's, and the cisterns are still filled with water. Syros, the central island of the Cyclades group, is particularly noted for its fine harbor; NAXOS, the largest, for its wine which pleased Bacchus; and MELOS, for the discovery of the "Venus of Milo," now in the Louvre. The ancient town of Melos lay beneath the modern town, KASTRO.

Corfu, "pearl of the Ionian," is a kind of vestibule to Greece on the west. Many of the charming natives speak Italian, and visitors especially enjoy themselves walking among the arbutus and myrtle, swimming, yachting, fishing, eating olives, and sampling the local wine. The view of the BAY OF CORFU from the old fort, with the little island of Pondikonisi in the foreground, is one of the hundreds of beautiful vistas. The island contains relatively few antiquities of note, yet is mentioned by Homer.

> Ulysses toward
> The gorgeous palace of Alcinous turned
> His steps, yet stopped and pondered ere he
>   crossed
> The threshold. For on every side beneath
> The lofty roof of that magnanimous king
> A glory shone as of the sun or moon.

YUGOSLAVIA

Yugoslavia was the battleground where West fought with East. The armies of Alexander the Great, Caesar, Charlemagne, Tatars, Crusaders, Turks, Napoleon, countless unnamed tribes and, recently, Germans and Russians have marched over this land and its people. The invaders have left their marks in great variety, each town and village possessing a tortuous history of its own. Geographically, the country is as varied as its peoples who, however, have one common trait; the constant and mostly unequal struggle has sharpened their character into one of fearless independence, evident even now in the contemporary news.

The country's same and also different seventeen million people are now joined together as the Federal People's Republic of Yugoslavia. There are six republics: Serbia, whose Belgrade is also the country's capital; Croatia, centering around Zagreb in the north; Slovenia with Ljubljana as its capital; Bosnia-Herzegovina with Sarajevo as its center; Macedonia, with Skoplje as its chief town in the south; and Montenegro with Titograd (formerly Podgorica) as its head.

Three Slavic languages are spoken (Serbo-Croatian, Slovenian, and Macedonian); two separate alphabets are used, the Cyrillic in the south and southeast and the Latin in the north and northwest; and there are three principal religions, Greek Orthodox, Catholic, and Mohammedan.

With its area of 95,558 square miles, a little less than the state of Oregon, Yugoslavia contains great variations in landscape and climate. The Alpine climate of the interior, with the great mountain ranges—Julian, Karawanken, and Savinja—produces dense pine, oak, and beech forests, fruit trees, and magnificent fields of wheat; while the Mediterranean coast is sub-tropical, with palm trees, agaves, oleanders, olives, lemons, and oranges. The country is also rich in ores and minerals, and its quicksilver is not unsymbolic of the strong-minded people, quick to defend their ideals, whether left or right of a seldom-popular middle road, either in politics or purely personal affairs.

Writers, poets, painters, potters, metal workers, weavers, musicians, dancers, and singers, the Yugoslavians are amazingly gifted and versatile. Theirs is also a great country of sport; a wide variety of game and fish in unspoiled mountains provide good hunting and fishing. Sailing off the Dalmatian coast, winter sports at Planica, or the international ski center where 120-meter jumps have been recorded, are other attractions visitors delight in sharing.

Belgrade, the Belleguarde of the Franks, a strategic fortress rising on the confluence of the Danube and Sava rivers, has been a military prize throughout its turbulent history. The city, a sort of political football, was stormed, kicked, carried, and held by successive armies of invaders. Not until the last century when it was retaken from the Turks by the Serbs who arose out of Sumadija, the region of wooded hills and mountains just south of it, did it become a significant part— the nerve center—of its people. As Oscar Davico, a local contemporary poet put it:

Ah, Serbia, lying among
Rebellions and orchards of dark plum
Among men in the fields of their birth
Among breast-swelling song
Ah, Serbia, born to become
The rebellion among the nations of the
  earth.
(Translated by Dorian Cooke)

Belgrade, the city, is quite new. It has a fine university, a cathedral, a palace, several theaters, good shops and attractive parks, including the deer park outside the city where stands the monument to Prince Michael on the spot of his assassination in 1868.

Following the Danube eastward, past the walls and high towers of the medieval Serbian fortresses of Golubac and Smederevo, is Djerdap, the Iron Gate, the great ravine where the river breaks through a narrow cleft between spurs of the Transylvanian Alps and the Balkan Mountains. The DJERDAP GAP is about seventy miles long and at its deepest part, at Kazan (the Kettle), the gorge is over two thousand feet deep. The Romans carved a road out of the rocky shore following the course of the entire gap. At its narrowest point the name of the Emperor Trajan, who was the builder, is carved in the rock above the river.

In the south, Macedonia, with its bare mountains and sterile rolling plains, still shows the effects of the heavy hand of the invader. It was taken from the Turks only in 1912. In its irrigated river valleys, maize, rice, cotton, tobacco, and opium are grown. Skoplje, on the Vardar, once the capital of the medieval Serbian emperor, Dushan, is now capital of the state. It still has a strong Turkish flavor—the "Kursumli Han" (an old Turkish hotel), baths, bazaars, a palace, and numerous mosques. There is also a great aqueduct built by Justinian, and nearby are some of the pre-Renaissance monas-

teries, with fine, astonishing frescoes. There is silkworm culture in this old capital of southern Serbia, silver filigree work, and an important opium market. Ohrid, near the Greek border, is on the lake where every year the eels come all the way from the Pacific to spawn. There is a quaint old monastery at the tip of the lake with remnants of both Roman and Byzantine landmarks in the neighborhood.

Along the entire length of the Adriatic coast a mountain range separates the interior from the seashore which is dotted with thousands of islands and many antique towns and cities. Kotor, in Montenegro, is situated at the end of the majestic GULF OF KOTOR and is surrounded with old ramparts. The Cathedral of Saint Triphun and the numerous Byzantine castles on the hills nearby are most impressive.

Risano and Perast, on the inner bay of the Gulf of Kotor, are Illyrian settlements of the Pirusti tribe. Later, Peter the Great sent the sons of Russian boyars to Perast for naval training. Ercegnovi, founded in the fourteenth century, is at the Boka Kotorska entrance and is a favorite wintering place. It was much fought over, being Turkish, Spanish and, later, Venetian.

Cetinje is reached by the serpentine road rising steeply from the sea. At one point this road reaches a height of more than 3000 feet, with one of the most breathtaking views in Europe. Cetinje is the ancient capital of Montenegro and this tiny spot in the Balkans was never conquered by any of the invaders, not even by Napoleon's army. Under its crags and black stony mountains, the bishop princes kept alive the last spark of free Christianity through the darkness of five hundred years of Turkish rule. Cetinje has a fine monastery, the palace of the late King Nicholas, a theater, a museum, and an old bell tower once used for a grisly display of the severed heads of Turks. Budva has a fourth century B.C. fortress, and the Podostrog Monastery where Bibles were printed only a few years after the Gutenberg discovery.

Cavtat, on the site of the ancient Epidaurus, is noted for its Roman remains and the beautiful mausoleum by Ivan Mestrovic, Yugoslavia's greatest sculptor. In a country with many types of native dress, the most colorful are worn around Cavtat; inland Trebinje, too, is as famous for its traditional folk dress as for its tobacco industry.

Of all the lovely Dalmatian towns, DUBROVNIK, "Pearl of the Adriatic," with a plethora of fortifications, villas, fountains, and sunny beaches, is the most enchanting and second only to Venice as a unique Adriatic sea-city. Founded in the seventh century, it remained under Byzantine rule until 1205; it was then Venetian until 1358. The town was an independent republic until Napoleon dissolved it. Its ramparts are as complete as those of the French Carcassonne, and without benefit of such intense restoration. Two gates guard the town from modern traffic, and within are such architectural gems as the Cathedral and the Church of Saint Blaise. The Renaissance palaces are lovely, too; and each year there are music and folklore festivals.

The whole coast line is studded with "rose-red cities, half as old as time," nearly all of them set within crenelated battlements. The islands, too, are fabulous for their number, for their beaches, vegetation, and antiquities. Korcula, off which Marco Polo was captured by the Genoese (and where the Moreska, a knightly folk dance commemorating a battle against the Moors, is performed every July 29) and Hvar, the Madeira of Yugoslavia, are two of the most famous. Korcula's Saint Mark's Church has paintings by Titian, Tintoretto, and Bellini. Around the town of Hvar are green groves of palms, aloes, figs, lemons, and oranges; and in it is a lovely twelfth-century cathedral. Farther into the Adriatic is the island of Bisevo with a "Blue Grotto" that rivals the one on Capri.

Salona, once the capital of Roman Dalmatia, has relics of a mausoleum, basilica, amphitheater, baths, and aqueduct; while SPLIT, right next to it, and the present capital, is a town that is and was a palace—that of Diocletian, completed in 305. The palace became the town, losing here a bit, gaining there another, through the centuries. Diocletian's original structure covered some ninety thousand square feet and was surrounded by huge walls, along the top of which ran a parapet. Towers strengthened and beautified the walls; and four great gates, with bronze grilles, closed the palace against all comers. Diocletian, after having been the bitterest of all the persecutors of Christianity, retired to this palace and much enjoyed his seclusion. "Could you but see," he wrote to a friend, "the cabbages I have raised with my own hands, you would never urge me to return to the purple." In the ninth century Diocletian's mausoleum became the Cathedral, and several centuries later a lovely decorated belfry in late Romanesque was added. The Temple of Jupiter was preserved as the baptistery. The bronze lions, an Egyptian sphinx in black marble and the Roman bas-reliefs are most impressive. Modern Split has a prosperous harbor and is gay with lovely beaches and with sailing and sports contests.

Northwest of Split is Trogir, on a little island linked by bridges to the mainland. Another perfect medieval city with narrow streets and many lovely old buildings, Trogir was founded in the fourth century B.C. by Syracusan Greeks. The monastery, Church of Saint Barba, the forts, Town Hall, palaces, and the Cathedral with Radovan's great portal, built in 1250, all amply prove how right Bernard Berenson was to say that "Trogir is a treasure house of art."

The island and town of RAB is Roman with many splendid later monuments including lovely old churches, an old castle, houses and palaces, many of which date back to the time of the Venetians. It is additionally popular with tourists for its good accommodations, wonderful swimming, and sailing in its bays. The larger island of Krk, to the north with its capital of the same name, is another layered city, centuries tiered upon centuries in its stones. Here the Crusaders came, and here is made some of the delicious red wine for which Dalmatia is still noted.

From Dubrovnik to Sarajevo, the train passes the long Popovo Polje, that is a lake only in winter, and the bogs of Gabela, whose waters contain hundreds of carp, eel, and marsh birds. Mostar, whose name comes from the old Turkish bridge built across the Neretva ("most" means bridge), has many lovely mosques, and is famous for its wines. Around here is cotton and tobacco country. Jablanica, where are new hydroelectric works, is at the foot of Mount Ivan, the watershed between the Black Sea and the Adriatic.

The Serbo-Croatian city of SARAJEVO, capital of Bosnia-Herzegovina, and Turkish for over four hundred years (until 1878), bristles with minarets. The old town with narrow streets, the Bosnian houses, Turkish bazaar, and the old orthodox church, is connected with the modern city by the Princip Bridge. This bridge was the scene of the assassination of Archduke Francis Ferdinand that lit the fuse to World War I, and is named after the national hero who died for the deed. To the north lies Jajce where Saint Luke, according to legend, lies buried in the ruined church dedicated to him. The city was once the residence of the kings of Bosnia; and the last of the line, beheaded by Mohammed II in 1463, is also buried there. Banja Luka, a little farther north, with its forty mosques and Roman remains, is the town from which Borberli, "The Dragon of Bosnia," set forth with spleen in 1831 on his holy war against the Turks. Like Jajce, it was many times a battlefield and is now surrounded by factories.

Inland is ZAGREB, commercial and cultural center of Croatia, and second largest Yugoslavian city. Founded on Roman remains, it is a happy mixture of old and new. The old winding streets, the eleventh-century fortress, and the Gothic Cathedral contrast with the broad streets, wide squares and parks, the modern office buildings, hotels and apartments of the new. Magnificent scenery and many of the best-known Yugoslavian spas mark the surrounding area.

The karst terrain of Gorski Kotar with its many rivers, now surfaced, now underground, its green meadows and wonderful pine forests, its excellent fishing, is ideal in summer. In the Platak region ski-runners can enjoy the vast snow field into June, while at the same time in Opatija the spring blossoms and the warm sea invites thousands of bathers to bask on the warm beaches. The highest mountains of the Gorski Kotar, Sneznik and Risnjak, are over 5000 feet high, and the main winter sports center is Delnice, above the deep valley of the Kupa River.

According to legend, Ljubljana was founded by Jason; it is built on the site of Augustus' city of Emona, devastated by the Huns in the fifth century. Today with many attractive old buildings and many modern ones, including factories, it is a scenic Alpine city and the capital of Slovenia. Within easy distance are the fourteen-mile-long Postojna grottoes (Postumia-Grotte), the largest stalactite and stalagmite caves in Europe, once visited by Dante, who refrained from "personalizing" the walls as Byron did the pillar at Sunium. In one of them, brightly illuminated for the occasion, a lively ball is held each year, where the young people dance traditional as well as modern dances.

Bled, the most famous Alpine resort in Yugoslavia, is in the romantic valley between the Julian Alps and the Karawanken Mountains. The glacial lake at BOHINJ, and the gorges of the Sava River Valley, as of the Logar Valley in the Savinja Alps, make this ideal climbing country. Slovenia has many farms and is famous for its livestock. Maribor, on the Drava, is a wine, wood, and fruit center; it is also noted as a tourist center both in winter and summer for mountain excursions. Near Ptuj, the Roman Poetuvium, with its great fortress dominating the whole countryside is one of the biggest aluminum factories in Europe.

All of Yugoslavia with its melting of East and West, its vital peoples, aged buildings, dramatic scenery, and sunny coastline, is still largely to be discovered by Americans. Radomir Konstantinovic, a young native poet, writes characteristically:

So I have come to your silent world of grass,
To the coast I did not encounter in my laughing days,
In all my long wanderings and my starlit revelling nights;
O give me good welcome to these rural ways. . . .

SPAIN

In Spain you are either burning hot or bitter cold; and measure, which for the French is a virtue, is for the Spaniard a vice called meanness. This most attractive, courteous, proud, strongly individual, and music-loving land shares with Portugal the Iberian Peninsula, from the Pyrenees at the French border to Gibraltar. The population of around 28,000,000 occupies an area of 196-607 square miles.

In history the Spaniards are best known to Americans for the period of Ferdinand and Isabella, when, on the threshold of their great power, Spain set sail for the Americas. On their home ground the dramatic Spaniards are also noted for the brilliance of the light and color of their country, and for the extremes to which both climate and people go. Visitors bring away vivid memories of their fierce bullfights and colorful matadors, their sinuous and briskly punctuated dancing, their fiestas and siestas, their stern-looking castles and lovely houses and patios. The European baroque, oriental Moorish, and international modern architecture are contrasts in the extreme.

The people in the north, most characteristically Iberian, are similar to those found also in Navarre and Gascony. From that side of the Pyrenees, in the eleventh and twelfth centuries, came the French architecture which is found, for instance, in the CATHEDRAL OF SANTIAGO DE COMPOSTELA. This important Romanesque building in Spain was certainly influenced by the Church of Saint Sernin of Toulouse. Santiago, formerly the capital of Galicia, is one of the most frequented pilgrim resorts in Europe; and in medieval times it was so crowded that the Milky Way was called "the road to Santiago." Saint James is supposed to be buried here, under the high altar of the Cathedral, which is made of jasper, alabaster, and eleven hundred pounds of silver. The Puerta de Platerías, at the south front of the transept, has twelfth-century reliefs; and the Pórtico de la Gloria, completed in 1188, is "one of the greatest glories of Christian art." Be-

sides the Cathedral, there are some other churches, a university, and lo mountains rising to over two thou

The paleolithic cave paintings ir Spain are similar to those found in the south of France. The most famous examples of all are at Altamira, near Santander, where natural looking animals are drawn on the walls. And near here, at Santillana, grotesque huntsmen and petticoated ladies are engagingly depicted on the walls of the old palaces. Santander is one of the two best-known summer resorts on the Bay of Biscay; San Sebastián is the other with its world-famous beach, La Concha (the shell). Here are motor, yacht, and horse races, Basque-ball games, and the best bullfighters from all Spain all summer long.

Guernica, a small town, nobly situated on the Mundaca, was the seat of the diet of Vizcaya, until the abolition of the Basque *fueros,* or special privileges, which, from the fourteenth century until recent times, provided for certain autonomous rights of the three Basque provinces and immunity from taxes and military service. The "song of the tree of Guernica" by José María Iparraguirro, a local ninetenth-century poet, is the Basque national anthem. The town, badly destroyed in 1937 during the Civil War, is the subject of one of expatriate Pablo Picasso's controversial paintings. The castle there once belonged to Napoleon III's brilliant and fashionable Empress Eugénie.

Near Burgos is the birthplace of the Cid, the name the Arabs gave to Rodrigo Diaz, Spain's legendary hero and mighty warrior of the eleventh century. The two hundred ballads about him indeed create "much doubt whether he achieved what is attributed to him," as the canon remarked in Cervantes' *Don Quixote.* Burgos, capital of one of the great forest provinces, is seat of an archbishop and the original of the climate that is "nine months winter and three months hell." (Boston borrowed the climate and comment, both.) The city stands on a 300-foot hill in the midst of monotonous plains; but the Gothic castle and other buildings are lovely, and the Gothic CATHEDRAL of white limestone, started in 1221 by the

English Bishop Maurice, is one of the great sights of Spain.

At the point between the Pyrenees and Aragon where the Ebro is crossed, is Saragossa, a city of over 200,000 inhabitants, in the middle of a waterless and treeless desert. From Miranda or historic Pamplona to Saragossa the way lies through the thirsty acres of ash-colored Aragon. The Ebro basin is barren gray, but the people, both men and women, wear wonderfully gay and exciting costumes, as if in defiance of their mournful landscape. Saragossa has a lovely bridge of seven arches, and the famed Cathedral of the Virgen del Pilar. Here during the second and third weeks in October are the *fallas* and big bullfights. The Audiencia is the former palace of the counts of Luna (now dukes) one of whom was Il Trovatore, of Verdi's opera.

The Roman city of Osca, with its province, now called Huesca by the Spaniards, was referred to by Plutarch as "an important town." The city has a late Gothic Cathedral, built on the site of a once-famous mosque. The main door is carved with fourteen colossal figures of apostles and saints, and there is an alabaster reredos to the high altar, the masterpiece of Damian Forment. Between here and the Pyrenees are old HILL TOWNS, such as Jaca, where the farmers pasture their cattle in the summer and eke out a hard existence in winter.

MONTSERRAT, the serrated, or sacred mountain, seen from a distance looks like a gigantic castle. It is outlined sharply on every side, and has strange rock formations, called *gistaus,* or "stone watchmen," by the Arabs. On three sides tremendous precipices make the summit inaccessible, but on the northeast there are both a road and a railway which scramble up the projecting terraces to the Benedictine monastery, founded in the tenth century. At 2910 feet, it is about two-thirds of the way up. Its great treasure is the small wooden Black Virgin, said to have been made by Saint Luke. Montserrat is also identified in medieval literature with Monsalvat, "the citadel of the Holy Grail." Above the monastery is the hermitage of San Jerónimo, nearly five thousand feet high,

with a grand view of the Catalonian mountains and plains. Saint Ignatius Loyola, after recovering from the wounds he received at the battle of Pamplona, stayed in Montserrat; and in nearby Manresa, which can be seen from San Jerónimo, he wrote his *Spiritual Exercises.*

Founded in the third century B.C., fabulous BARCELONA is the largest city in Spain, with the possible exception of expanding Madrid. Cupped within a hilly amphitheater facing the Mediterranean Sea, it has Rome's latitude. The old city, walled until the 1860's, is now surrounded by the new, and the place of the wall has been taken by great avenues, or *rondas,* which in the northeast combine with the park. Don Quixote called wealthy Barcelona "the seat of courtesy, the haven of strangers, the refuge of the distressed, the mother of the valiant, the champion of the wronged, the abode of true friendship, unique both in beauty and situation." Named for Hamilcar Barca, the Carthaginian, the old city has many Roman remains. The Ramblas, the main street of the old town, are delightful, with flower and bird markets. The old Cathedral of Santa Eulalia with its magnificent stained glass windows, is the supreme example of Spanish Gothic. One of the chapels contains the statue of Christ carried by Don John of Austria at the battle of Lepanto.

Other interesting buildings in Barcelona are the Archivo General, built for the Emperor Charles V, and the Casa Consistorial, or Town Hall, dating from 1369, with beautiful ceilings and *ajimez* windows of a type peculiar to Catalonia and Valencia. The university was founded in 1430, and down by the harbor is the little house of Cervantes, No. 33 Paseo de Colon. The city's 15,000-seat ring is usually filled to overflowing with bullfight fans; another great attraction is Basque-ball (pelota); so is the opera, during January and February. The PUEBLO ESPAÑOL contains interesting examples of different types of Spanish architecture. Picasso, Salvador Dali, Pablo Casals, and many other famous Spaniards are from Barcelona or from its sunny, fruit-growing environs.

Down the Catalan coast is Castellón de la

Plana, which James I captured from the Moors. The railroad from Barcelona goes through it en route to Valencia. Belonging, respectively, to the Iberians, Greeks, Carthaginians, Romans, Visigoths, and Moors, the Valencians are a "very mixed race." The city itself, cosmopolitan, gay, sunny, glistening white on the blue Mediterranean, has a wonderful museum with Velázquez, Dürer, Goya, and modern paintings; interesting Roman and Moorish remains; and a lovely thirteenth-century Cathedral. This is a city for exquisite native silks and *azulejos* (tiles). Rice, oranges, and many fruits grown in the neighboring districts are exported. The music is good in the fall to spring season, as it is in Barcelona, and everyone has a wonderful time at the *fallas* of Saint Joseph in mid-March when bonfires are lit and fireworks explode in every direction.

Within fifty-five miles west of Madrid is the walled city of AVILA, a castle unto itself and capital of a province in the midst of the high Sierras. Standing nearly four thousand feet high on a flat ridge which springs abruptly from a treeless plain, it is surrounded on three sides by mountains. The whole city, including the Walls, still perfectly preserved with nine gates and eighty-six towers, is built of beige colored granite. The battlemented Cathedral, with its two strong towers, looks more like a fortress than a church. There is a monument to Saint Theresa ("I need no rest; what I need is crosses"), and a convent is built on the site where the saint was born.

The best Roman remains in Spain are at Segovia, notably the aqueduct, built under Augustus and restored by Trajan. The Cathedral at Segovia is a light, airy Gothic basilica, and the magnificent ALCAZAR, rebuilt in 1352-1358, is the outstanding example of an old Castilian castle. It resisted the Comuneros in 1520. More recent history was made at the Toledo Alcazar, defended against the Republicans in the last Civil War. The telephone conversation between a father and his son, with its terse ending, is classic: "Now you must get ready to die," the general said. "Yes, Father, I will," replied the boy, who was then taken out and shot.

TOLEDO, once capital of Spain, and center of early struggles of the Church, is a savagely beautiful town, crowded with buildings on narrow streets. Lope de Vega, who wrote some 1000 books, plays, and poems, stopped here in his wanderings; and El Greco, fresh from Venice, stopped to paint his greatest works. (His "Storm over Toledo" is one of the most popular oils in New York's Metropolitan Museum.) Toledo is Roman, Visigothic, Saracen, and Christian in turns and all at once. The best churches are two former synagogues, built in Moslem style, Santa Maria la Blanca and the Transito, and a small mosque, El Cristo de la Luz, built in 922.

The city of the Inquisition, Toledo was also a center of Arabic and Jewish studies. The Cathedral, with the Puerta de los Leones, and glorious fifteenth-century stained glass windows, dates from 1227. In Santo Tomé is El Greco's "Burial of Count Orgaz," his greatest painting, and in the museum hang several others of his works. There is also a weapon factory where Toledo blades are still made, but they are not what they were in the old days, when a Toledo sword would roll up like a watch spring. Gun barrels are made here too, but no longer from the mule-shoe and horseshoe nails which gave Toledo steel its distinctive marking.

The youngest of the great cities of Spain is Madrid, with its bad climate and excellent university. Largely rebuilt since the Civil War, the city everywhere has well-designed new apartment houses, new business premises, new ministries, and whole new suburbs of five- and six-story houses which have grown up around it. The Prado, one of the world's finest museums, houses most of the work of Goya, a magnificent collection of Titians, Tintorettos, and Rubens', over forty great Velázquezs, and a roomful of El Grecos. The Puerta del Sol, the largest and most vital plaza in Madrid; the Goya frescoes in the Church of San Francisco, where the artist is buried; the Plaza Mayor; Retiro Park with its rose gardens; Aranjuez, the Spanish Versailles, with its pompous eighteenth-century palace and the gardens of La Isla (on a comparable scale to the magnificent palace and gardens of La Granja, near

Segovia) where Schiller's nightingales sang so beautifully; and the dark Escorial, Philip II's palace-monastery, are sights to be seen in and around the city.

The ground plan of the ESCORIAL (1563-1584), designed by Juan de Bautista de Toledo, represents the griddle on which Saint Lawrence was roasted. "Turn me over," he told his executioners; "that side is done enough." Solid, grand, and gloomy, it seems to rise directly from the Guadarrama Mountains. The high altar of the Panteón de los Reyes, the burial vault of the Spanish monarchs, is directly above the bodies of the dead kings. Both the church and the sacristy contain admirable oil paintings. There is also a lovely small picture gallery and a wonderful library. The dark cells where Philip II lived were decorated with the "Deadly Sins" by Hieronymus Bosch. Among his "Seven," in the picture now hanging in the Prado, are *anger* with drunkards, *avarice* with a bribe-minded judge, *lust* with two amorous couples in a tent; there is a wonderful *heaven* scene, and all *hell* breaks loose in the lower left corner with devils pulling or pronging everyone in sight. In contrast to the work of Bosch, El Greco's MARTYRDOM OF SAINT MAURICE is sublimely conceived and, with his other masterpieces in Toledo and Madrid, are alone worth a visit to Spain.

If the Escorial is one of the great of Christian monuments in Spain, the ALHAMBRA is certainly the greatest of the secular Moslem monuments in Europe. Granada, a city of around 170,000 inhabitants, is situated at the base of two mountain spurs, one of which is the Albaicín, or falconers hill, and the other the Alhambra. During his visit, Longfellow wrote:

> Granada by its winding stream,
>   The city of the Moor;
> And there the Alhambra still recalls
>   Aladdin's palace of delights.

The family of the Nasrides, whose power was established by Mohammed I, in 1232, ruled Granada for 250 years. The finest parts of the Alhambra were built by Mohammed V (1334-1391). He completed the Court of the Myrtles and the COURT OF THE LIONS with the twelve beasts bearing the central fountains. The elms in the Alhambra Park were brought by the Duke of Wellington in 1812. Innumerable nightingales live among them, and here it is always green. By the Gate of Judgment, used as an informal court of justice by the Moors, one enters the palace. "The thin and fragile marble columns, on which rest large masses of masonry, are an imitation of tent-poles; the brilliant colors of the arabesque ornamentation are an echo of the gay patterns of the carpets with which Arab tents were draped." The Hall of the Two Sisters, whose honeycombed roof has at least five thousand cells, with red, blue, and green *azulejos,* is enchanting. Washington Irving loved best the Mirador de Daraxa, with its colored crystals. The baths also are exquisite, with slender columns and mosaic flooring. The Generalife, the Moorish summer palace, is a series of courtyards giving on to "gardens, wherein waters flow," which is the Koran's description of Paradise.

Granada, the last stronghold of the Moors in Spain, was captured in 1492 by Ferdinand and Isabella, whose tombs are to be seen in the Cathedral. The city is an iridescent mixture of East and West, of modern and ancient, with lovely views of the snow-capped Sierra Nevada. On the Sacro Monte hill, some two thousand GITANOS live in caves. These gypsies proudly trace their ancestry back to the Pharaohs of Egypt, dress in colorful costumes, and dance magnificently.

The Cathedral at Cordova, formerly the chief mosque of the Moors, is second in size only to the one in Mecca among Moslem mosques, and is the greatest example of Islamic religious art in Europe. Nearly nine hundred columns still remain, some of marble, others of porphyry or jasper, and of all styles. There are nineteen aisles. Of the prayer niches, only the Third Mihrab remains, covered with mosaics, its walls paneled with richly carved marble.

The most famous festivals of any town in Spain are held at SEVILLE, though Holy Week is also very impressively celebrated in Toledo and Madrid. The Seville processions are more colorful than anywhere else in Europe, and nowhere else is there the Dance of the Six Boys, dressed in costumes of Philip III's time, in front of the High Altar of the Cathedral. The magnificent Easter FERIA (fair) is a top-ranking event in Spain; everyone dresses up, and BULLFIGHTS and flamenco dancing add to the general excitement and color. Corpus Christi, too, and All Saints are splendidly celebrated. Seville owes nothing to its setting, which is perfectly flat and dull, yet it is one of the gayest cities in the world: nearly every house seems shining and white, every space tree-planted and green. The climate is marvelous most of the time and roses bloom nearly all year round. The old saying goes, "Who has not seen Seville has seen nothing." Velázquez and Murillo were born in the city and the Murillos in the Fine Arts Museum are among his best. The Moorish Alcazar and LA GIRALDA, the twelfth-century minaret, are lovely; and the light and airy Cathedral adjoining the Giralda is one of the largest, richest, and finest Gothic cathedrals anywhere. The building, begun in 1402, was finished in 1519. From the river it looks like a high-pooped and beflagged ship. In the old days the great bells were pealed on festival days by colorfully dressed youths who willingly risked their lives as they hung, and swung, by straps attached to the clappers. The Duke of Alba's magnificent Casa de las Dueñas is most certainly worth seeing, and so are the many lovely private houses with luxuriously planted patios.

Málaga, on the Mediterranean, with its Cathedral and Moorish castle, is situated in one of the most fertile parts of Spain. It was a Phoenician port (and resort), and both in Roman and Arab times the town was famous as a depot for salt fish. From the Málaga coast, with its picturesque little towns such as FUENGIROLA, Torremolinos, and Marbella, ideal for summer and winter vacations, the northernmost tip of Africa can sometimes be seen.

A lot happened to CADIZ after Pytheas studied the tides for the Greeks; and Juvenal and Martial, impressed with its "dancing girls," called it "Cadiz the joyous." At the end of Roman domination the Visigoths almost literally threw Cadiz into the sea; all that remains of the ancient masonry has lain at the bottom of the harbor ever since. The occupation of the Moors lasted 551 years, until Alfonso X of Castile marched in and rebuilt the city. Its great wealth began through trade with the new American colonies. Elizabeth I of England, who feared the power of Spain, gloated when Drake "singed the Spanish king's beard," burning all the ships in sight. In 1800 Nelson bombarded Cadiz; in 1810-1812 the French besieged it (while it was the capital of all Spain outside Napoleon's empire); and in 1812 the Cortes formed the famous liberal constitution. Cadiz has always bobbed up after each misfortune, like a cork in its own harbor, and today presents its sunny, whitewashed face to the sea. The city was the birthplace of one of the greatest of modern composers, Manuel de Falla. Cadiz has a bull ring, the San Fernando Arsenal, theaters, a fine museum and Cathedral, and many churches, including the former church of Santa Catalina (now an asylum) where Murillo fell to his death from a scaffold before completing his painting of "Saint Catherine."

Palos de la Frontera is the port from which Columbus sailed on August 3, 1492, with his three small vessels, the *Santa Maria,* the *Pinta* and the *Niña,* and to which he returned on March 15, 1493. The town of Huelva was colonized by the Romans and still has their aqueduct, as well as the monastery where Columbus stayed, a statue to him, and several churches. In the same maritime province is MANZANILLA, a picturesque old town famous for its wines.

The colorful Balearic Islands are only a forty-minute flight from the east coast of Spain, or overnight by boat. The golden island of Majorca is largest of the group and lovely PALMA is its capital. There are many worth-while old buildings, lovely modern villas, hotels, beaches, marble quarries, and caves. Everywhere the scenery is superb and the light wine is delicious. The brandy (what is left of it) gets exported. Imported were Chopin, whose house can be seen, and his friend and companion, George Sand. Minorca too is justly praised, and so, as George Eliot said, is most of

Broadbreasted Spain, leaning with equal
   love
(A calm earth-goddess crowned with corn
   and vines)
On the mid sea that moans with memories
And on the untravelled ocean, whose vast
   tides
Pant dumbly passionate with dreams of
   youth.

PORTUGAL

"What Heaven hath done for this delicious land," exclaimed Byron, visitor in a country that lives poetry, lives courtesy, and at times is perhaps even more colorful in its customs and costumes than Spain.

In this "unitary and corporative republic" lying between Spain and the Atlantic, three hundred and sixty miles long and one hundred and eighty wide, live nearly 9 million people. From Lisbon, its capital, voyagers have sailed to carry Portugal's name across the world, for the Portuguese are a nation of adventurers as well as poets. Some were both. Jeronymo Corte-Real, brother of the Gaspar who discovered Labrador and opened Newfoundland to Portuguese fishermen in 1501, was himself a soldier and seafarer. He wrote *O Segundo cerco de Diu,* epic of the adventurers of his day. In the same century, Luiz Vaz de Camoëns served in Africa and India, and swam ashore after a shipwreck off the coast of Cambodia, carrying above his head *Os Lusíadas,* penned with "the charm of the Odyssey and the magnificence of the Aeneid," and which many in Portugal seem to know by heart.

Equally famous was Vasco da Gama, the first to find a sea route around Africa to India; then there was Pedro Alvares Cabral, who stumbled upon Brazil; Juan Cabrillo, who found California in 1542; and the great Magellan.

LISBON, one of the most attractive cities in Europe, is welcoming and friendly, and the seven hills are *real* ones that take hard climbing. So many of the houses and pavings are covered in beautifully colored tiles, and so much bravely colored washing is hung from window to window across the narrow streets, and there are so many flower sellers everywhere that the traveler's impression is of looking into a kaleidoscope; every moment there is a new impression of jeweled light. Lisbon is for the most part a vivid and strikingly clean city, and a prosperous and busy one, with excellent shopping, museums and libraries, a good national ballet, opera, and symphony. The Avenida da Liberdade is fashionable and the Alameda de São Pedro de Alcantara is a delicious shady walk, with a flower garden and lovely views. Down by the harbor and in the fish market one can spend hours watching the colorful natives and the fascinating boats. From Lisbon sailed the ill-fated Spanish Armada, here too the people welcomed Vasco da Gama home after his eventful voyage.

The Sé Patriarchal, a cathedral founded in 1150 by Alfonso I and once a mosque, was mostly destroyed in the 1755 earthquake which demolished so many of Portugal's old buildings. In one of the chapels is the tomb of Lisbon's patron saint, Saint Vincent. Also in the Alfama, or old town, is the Castle São Jorge, a Moorish citadel, and Nossa Senhora da Graça with the tomb of Alfonso de Albuquerque, and the legendary "wonder-working statue of Christ." On the outskirts of the city is the very impressive BELEM TOWER, characteristically Portuguese (Manueline) and built in the early sixteenth century to defend the Tagus.

Vasco da Gama and the poet Camoëns are supposedly buried in the lovely Jeronymos convent and church, founded in 1499, which commemorate the explorer's discoveries, and the tomb of Catherine of Braganza, wife of Charles II of England, is here. The beautiful cloisters and gateway designed by the great Manueline architect João de Castilho are unaltered, and here are the lifelike figure of Saint Jerome ("I am waiting for it to speak to me," said Philip II) and the stone elephant-borne tombs of the kings and queens of Portugal. The royal coach houses at Belem, the first in the world, are a curiosity, and Queluz, with its royal palace, built as a copy of Versailles by King John V, is completely enchanting. Crossing the Alcantara Valley, the great eighteenth-century AQUEDUCT of Aguas Livres (the older of two) brings water to the city over its thirty-two high arches.

Estoril, fifteen miles from Lisbon, is a fashionable coastal resort, with wonderful golf, tennis, swimming, and a casino. Quite different is SINTRA (Cintra) which Byron, who lived there for a while, called "a glorious Eden," and elsewhere sung of it in *Childe Harold*. Sintra is buried among woods of evergreen, oaks, cork trees, and umbrella pines. In the city is the royal palace, charmingly furnished and as famous for its conical kitchen chimneys as for its dining room with King John's magpie ceiling. Here the birds chant "Por Bem" from their scrolls, immortalizing the king's remark ("In Honor") when his proud English queen, Philippa of Lancaster, caught him embracing a pretty maid of honor there. The Castle of Pena, "a romanticist's version of a medieval castle," built by King Consort Ferdinand of Saxe-Coburg-Gotha in the nineteenth century on the rocky peak of the Serra, one of the highest in the region, has a unique view of the sea and the province of Estremadura. The ruined castle of the Moors is nearby. Amongst the richest vegetation in Europe is Sintra's great park with an overwhelming profusion of camellias, eucalyptus, cork trees, evergreen oaks, rhododendron, azaleas, magnolias, and, everywhere and in all colors, cinerarias. Myrtle, rosemary, and roses are abundantly wild in this landscaped area of lakes, forests, and mountains, the finest natural garden on the Iberian Peninsula, certainly, and perhaps of anywhere in the world.

Impressive, too, is the Pinhal de Leiria, the large pine woods planted by King Denis (1279-1325) between the beautiful city of LEIRIA and the ocean. Leiria has a castle built by the first king of Portugal in 1135; it is also noted as the home town of the poet Francisco Rodrigues Lobo, after whom the main square is named, and for the establishment of the first Portuguese printing press in 1466.

The well-cultivated countryside of Portugal is tremendously varied, between the lagoons of the Tagus and the grain- and cork-growing provinces of the Alentejo, the mountains of the north, and the many lovely valleys of the Tagus and the Douro. OPORTO (Porto) is on the Douro. This crowded commercial, industrial, and capital city of north Portugal has a large harbor with interesting and varied craft, two iron bridges (one built by Eiffel of Paris), narrow streets with traders on donkeys or in ox-driven carts mingling with the modern traffic, and exotic parks and gardens. Here aloes and citrus trees grow naturally with all the common plants and flowers of northern Europe. The neighboring vineyards too are legendary, for Oporto made its fortune with wine and gives its name to the only authentic "Port" in the world. In the midst of glorious hillside scenery it is still common to find barefoot natives crushing their purple harvests—to music, furthermore, just as they have always done since anyone can remember.

Oporto has fine churches and a Cathedral, a museum, opera, and bull ring. It has memories of Wellington who drove out the French in 1809 and ate with relish the dinner that had been prepared for Napoleon's Marshal Soult, and of sedan chairs which were a common sight right up to the present century. Both these and the plaid materials still worn by the Portuguese were the result of contact with the British, who did much to develop the port industry. Besides its wine, Oporto busies itself with the fishing industry (sardines are legion), pottery, cotton, silk, leather and jewelry, rivaling Lisbon, its great competitor in the south—whose inhabitants these northerners, characteristically outspoken and with a charming drawl, call "a set of idle chatterers."

Coimbra, on the Lisbon-Oporto railway, was Moorish before Ferdinand I and the Cid captured it in 1064 and capital of the country until 1260. Six kings were born there. The university, one of the oldest in Europe, shuttled between Lisbon and Coimbra, but is now firmly and beautifully established in

Coimbra. The city, with its many interesting buildings, stands on a series of magnificent hills spread out like an amphitheater. In the Quinta das Lágrimas, the well-laid-out park, is the famous "Fonte dos Amores" where Dom Pedro's beloved Inés de Castro was stabbed to death in 1355. Coimbra is also where Luiz Vaz de Camoëns was born in 1524, and where, as a youth, he studied.

Much of Portugal's prosperity comes from the excellence of its maritime fishing industry; few fish markets in the world are more prosperous. Typical of the small coastal towns and villages, but one of the most colorful, is NAZARÉ. The market square with its patterns of tile, fishing craft in dry dock, open-air markets, and gayly colored balconied houses is altogether delightful. The fishermen, in their plaid trousers or shirts and long knitted tasseled caps (convenient for holding a pipe and tobacco), shove off from shore into the dangerous breakers for their daily catch or mend their nets on the sandy beach. The crescent-shaped boats are brightly painted, many with "eyes" in their bows to help them look for fish. At Fatima, a little over a hundred miles northeast of Lisbon, regularly twice a year pilgrims pay tribute to the little shepherds, Francisco, Lucia, and Jacinta, whose story of the appearance of the Virgin no one would at first believe. At Batalha, another much visited place, there are a lovely fourteenth-century Gothic monastery church and Founder's Chapel, an octagon upheld by eight pillars.

Here John I and his wife, Philippa, rest on eight lions, and here the royal cloisters display the lotus motifs which symbolize Portugal's great interest and achievements in the East.

At Alcobaça the shops and sunny market place are filled with lovely faïence, rugs, carpets, homespun textiles, and tantalizing fruits. The abbey, founded in 1148 by the Cistercians, was one of the largest in the world, and the CHURCH is clean, airy, and vast. "The tumult of the square, the shouts of the market-women, the braying of the donkeys, the bleating of the tethered kids, does not penetrate into the empty halls, the warm, flower-decked courtyards, the echoing corridors paved with tombstones," Doré Ogrizek writes under the same spell as the countless others who have visited the tombs of Inés de Castro and Dom Pedro (among the finest achievements of medieval sculpture), which adorn this church at Alcobaça. Here also others of the Portuguese monarchy are enshrined where the "smell of warm box trees" drifts into the threefold nave and the sun shines gloriously on the symbols of eternity.

Here in Portugal is the occidental extremity of Europe, as in Norway was the most northern, in Sicily the most southern, in Hagia Sophia and Istanbul across the Aegean, the end or the beginning of the East.

Europe is a way of life, a way of thought, and last, but certainly not least, a way of prayer.

GREECE

Fritz Henle

Athens. The Erechtheum (c. 421–407 B.C.), on the Acropolis. Porch of the Maidens.

Athens. The Corinthian Temple of Olympian Zeus, started by Antiochus and finished by Hadrian

The Parthenon (Temple of Athena) on the Acropolis, built under Pericles' direction in the Vth century B.C.

Evzones guard the King's Palace and the Tomb of the Unknown Soldier in Athens.

Charles Trieschman

Below: The Ionic Vth-century Temple of Athena Nike on the Acropol

Ewing Gallowe

Martin Hürlimann

Apollo from the Temple of Zeus, in the Olympia Museum.

The tholos and temple ruins on the Marmaria at Delphi, seat of the great temple and oracle of Apollo. *Below:* Mount Olympus, Thessaly-Macedonia.

Bosshard

...oung shepherd in hilly Thrace. *Below:* Athos, Macedonia. Saint Denis Monastery, one of twenty such ...ommunities on the Holy Mountain.

Galloway

Ewing Galloway

Below: Kastro on Melos, the island where the "Venus of Milo" was discovere[

posite: Corfu. Two tiny islands in the bay, seen from the fort.

Sauvageot

ne of the statues on the Avenue of Lions, Delos.

Kostich

The Iron Gate at Djerdap Gap on the Danube, within one hundred miles of Belgrad

ew from "Villa Scheherazade" in fortified Dubrovnik, most picturesque Dalmatian coastal
y. *Below:* Gulf of Kotor, Montenegro.

S.T.

219

Comb.

Split, Dalmatia seaport, especially noted for its fine harbor and the third-century palace of Diocletian.

Left: Rab (Arbe), beautiful island town and resort off the coast of Croatia, has Roman and Venetian remains.

Opposite: Sarajevo, capital of Bosnia-Herzegovina. The town, with its hundred mosques and Turkish bazaar, was the scene of Archduke Ferdinand's assassination that led to World War I.

Kostich

W. Suschitzky

221

Kosti

Zagreb, thriving inland capital of Croatia.

Left: Children in folk costume at Bohinj, Slovenia, near the Italian border.

Opposite: The Cathedral at Santiago, La Coruña, legendary burial place of Saint James, and center of great pilgrimages to northern Spain.

Kostich

222

In the cathedral at Burgos, capi‑
tal of Old Castile, and now of the
province of the same name. The
Cid, Spanish national hero, was
born near Burgos.

Left: Hill town and pasture in
Huesca.

Opposite: Old Spanish architec‑
ture in the Pueblo Español at
Barcelona.

Zerkowitz

225

Montserrat, near Barcelona. "Stone watchmen." Near here is the chapel of the "Black Virgin." *Below:* Avila, highest cathedral city in Europe, and birthplace of Saint Theresa.

Bernard G. Silberstein

ne of the spires of the spectacular fourteenth-century Castilian Alcazar at Segovia.

The magnificent "Martyrdom of Saint Maurice," painted by El Greco for the Escorial.

The Escorial, Philip II's palace-monastery near Madrid. *Below:* Toledo, former capital of Spain.

Fritz Hen

Brassai

Gay and beautiful Seville. *Above:* View from the Giralda. *Left:* At the *feria* (fair), a leading annual event in Spain. *Opposite, top:* A bullfight in the arena.

Opposite: "The Court of the Lions" in the Alhambra, the Moorish palace at Granada.

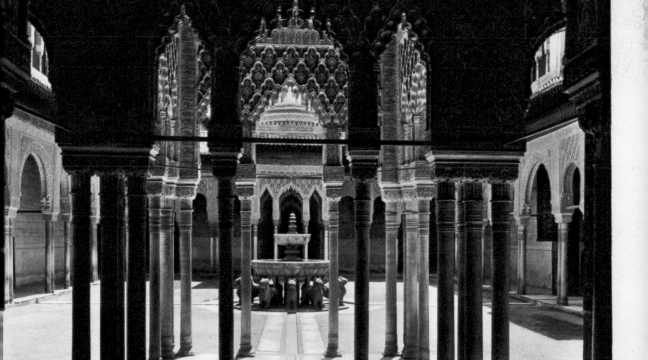

Roger Coster

Gitana dancer on the Sacro Monte hill, Granada. *Opposite, top:* Fuengirola, Mediterranean town near Málaga. *Opposite:* Cadiz, seen from the watch tower.

232

Kindel

Ewing Galloway

Kindel

Manzanilla, in Huelva, maritime province from which Columbus sailed.

Palma, capital of Majorca, Chopin and George Sand stayed in this largest of the Balearic Islands.

Ewing Krainin

Lisbon. General view over the capital, and (*below*) the aqueduct of Aguas Livres, which brings water across the Alcantara Valley.

Ewing Krainin

PORTUGAL

wing Galloway

Casa de Portugal

Oporto (Porto) on the Douro, center of the port wine trade.

Right: Belem Tower on the Tagus, outside Lisbon. The Manueline architecture is a cross between Gothic and Moorish.

Opposite, top: Sintra (Cintra), west of Lisbon, praised by Byron and Camoëns. The royal palace is at distant right.

Opposite: Leiria. The castle (on hill), built in 1135 by the first king of Portugal, figured in the wars against the Moors.

Fritz Henle

pposite and above: Nazaré, Estremadura, is most characteristic of the Portuguese fishing vil-
ges. The plaids, long caps, and crescent-shaped boats (sometimes painted with eyes to help
eir owners look for fish) are typical.

Fritz Henle

Prayer in the beautiful church at Alcobaça, Estremadura. Here lie the tombs of Dom Pedro and Inés de Cast

INDEX

241

242